PRAISE FOR *Seeking Rapture*

"Any wife, mother or daughter can find herself in the moments of Kathryn Harrison's *Seeking Rapture:* from Harrison's quiet survey of the comforting clutter in her children's room to her desperate lifelong search for her own mother's approval. Perhaps most refreshing is Harrison's amusingly self-deprecating but insightful voice that weaves disparate moments into a story of personal growth. . . . Harrison writes here with the careful details, full characters and growing tension of a novelist, yet allows meaning to emerge quietly as the stories layer upon one another to form a greater whole. . . . *Seeking Rapture* is an exploration of interiors and exteriors. And, thankfully, [Harrison] allows us to join her on her journey, as a woman and as a writer."

—*Rocky Mountain News*

"Worthwhile . . . 'Renewal' [is] a funny account of how [Harrison] helped her grandmother cheat her way to success on her driving test, and 'What Remains' [is] a fascinating essay about artifacts of the dead, from relics of the saints to Kurt Cobain's bloody guitar."

—*People*

"Harrison remains a master of her craft, with musings that are lyrical, insightful, and haunting."

—*Entertainment Weekly*

"It's [Harrison's] fierce devotion to her absent mother that gives this book its shimmering grace."

—*Organic Style*

"Poignant glimpses into the life of a survivor."

"Harrison's affinity for vivisecting the soft underbelly of social mores . . . is vividly apparent in this series of autobiographical essays. . . . The most evocative piece, the title essay, shows Harrison at her thoughtful, provocative best, mindful of the flaws and desires within everyone."

ABOUT THE AUTHOR

KATHRYN HARRISON is the author of the novels *The Seal Wife,*
The Binding Chair, Poison, Exposure, and *Thicker Than Water.* She
has also written a memoir, *The Kiss,* a travel memoir, *The Road to
Santiago,* and a biography, *Saint Thérèse of Lisieux.* Her personal
essays have appeared in *The New Yorker, Harper's Magazine,* and
other publications. She lives in New York with her husband, the
novelist Colin Harrison, and their children. She can be reached at
thebindingchair@yahoo.com.

SEEKING RAPTURE

SEEKING
RAPTURE
scenes from a woman's life

KATHRYN HARRISON

RANDOM HOUSE TRADE PAPERBACKS

NEW YORK

2004 Random House Trade Paperback Edition
Copyright © 2003 by Kathryn Harrison

All rights reserved under International and Pan-American Copyright
Conventions. Published in the United States by Random House Trade
Paperbacks, an imprint of The Random House Publishing Group,
a division of Random House, Inc., New York, and simultaneously
in Canada by Random House of Canada Limited, Toronto.

RANDOM HOUSE TRADE PAPERBACKS and colophon are
registered trademarks of Random House, Inc.

This work was originally published in hardcover by Random House
Publishing Group, a division of Random House, Inc., in 2003.

Library of Congress Cataloging-in-Publication Data

Harrison, Kathryn.
Seeking rapture : scenes from a woman's life / Kathryn Harrison.
p.   cm.
ISBN 0-8129-7205-8
1. Harrison, Kathryn.   2. Novelists, American—20th century—
Biography.   3. Women—United States—Biography.   I. Title.

PS3558.A67136 Z477 2003
813'.54—dc21   2002031620
[B]

Random House website address: www.randomhouse.com

Printed in the United States of America

246897531

Book design by Casey Hampton

WITH THANKS TO SARAH, WALKER, AND JULIA,
without whom this book could not exist

The world will freely offer itself to you to be unmasked,
it has no choice, it will roll in ecstasy at your feet.

— FRANZ KAFKA

CONTENTS

SEEKING RAPTURE

THE CHILDREN'S ROOM

The children are young enough so that the passage between our two bedrooms is still umbilical, a door through which I travel nightly once or twice, between midnight and dawn, sometimes more often. Summoned by a cry, impelled by a worry or nightmare of my own, I don't wake fully in the journey from our bed to Walker's (nine steps) or Sarah's (fourteen). I kneel beside whichever child I've come to comfort; sometimes I let my cheek rest on the foot of the bed and fall back into my dreams. When I rouse myself, minutes or hours later, I am cold, stiff, confused. The night-light, which seems so weak at bedtime that it fails to illuminate the cars and dolls and blocks underfoot, dazzles my just-opened eyes. The entire room is gold and glowing, and I can see each eyelash curled against his cheek, count the pale freckles on her nose.

Boy and girl, they are still young enough to share this large room that adjoins our bedroom, the room that, innocent of children, my husband and I imagined would be a library. After all, it has a whole wall of floor-to-ceiling book-cases. When we moved into this brownstone in Brooklyn, I transferred novels and poems and essays from their boxes (packed as they had been shelved, alphabetically) directly into the empty cases. At last, here was a home with built-in shelves! A fireplace, and furniture inherited from my mother's mother—antique steamer trunks, mahogany chairs and desk, a chaise longue for more desultory study—contributed to our literary aspirations for the space. Now only the chaise remains. All but the top four shelves are emptied of grown-up books and filled with toys, picture books, art supplies. I have removed novels and essays, poems and histories as I have needed to, in response to our children's ability to reach and climb. I carried them upstairs and stacked them, "A"s and "M"s and "Z"s all jumbled together and furred with dust. This was the way the room was transformed from library to nursery: book by book, shelf by shelf, chair by chair. I wonder if it is by equally small increments that we become parents, as our children claim another and another sinew of devotion.

Sarah's arrival was followed by that of her crib. Hundred-spindled, made of fruitwood, it displaced two chairs and the desk. When she woke at two or at four and called me to her, I stumbled from our bed to the crib and reached over its tall side. I took her into my arms and took us both into the chaise, where we ultimately fell asleep together, my nipple still in her mouth.

Long before she stopped nursing, our daughter began acquiring *things,* many of them. The baby swing and the toy chest nudged the steamer trunks to the living room; a rocking chair replaced the last of its immobile colleagues. Colin and I bought a craft table so small that even carefully folded onto the matching stools we cannot coax our humped knees under its surface, now covered with sedimentary layers of adhesives and pigment. Before Sarah was three, she became enamored of Play-Doh, paste, poster paint, acrylic paint, glitter paint, oil paint, and Magic Markers. In short order, she acquired a glue gun; a glutinous, slippery, shiny gunk called Gak; Silly Putty; plaster of Paris; a machine that employs centrifugal force to splatter paint onto whirling cards; and a little brother—all of which arrivals encouraged the exchange of the pink and mauve Oriental rug for a nearly wall-to-wall Stainmaster in a practical shade of dark blue.

Three years old, the carpet already wears its history. People who do not have children will give other people's children the sort of gifts their parents never buy, hence the popularity of bachelor uncles and courtesy aunts. Hence the glue gun and Gak. I drew the line at hot paraffin and hid the candle-making kit, but, still, we paint and draw and mold and glue a lot—every day—and the more ambitious art projects do leave incidental impressions, stains, gouges. The rocking chair, I noticed recently, has been decorated with stickers and wobbly stripes of red and green around its arms and along the sides of its seat. It has older scars, of course; this rocker was in my childhood bedroom, and before that in my mother's. It has been glued and clamped, screwed and reglued by both my grandfather and my husband.

The baby swing and the changing table, the crib and the walker are gone now, and each of the children has what is called a "youth" bed—smaller than a twin and closer to the floor. At five, Sarah is nearly too large for hers, but she's not ready to part with it. She hated to lose its predecessor, the crib, which we tactfully dismantled long before her brother's arrival and only after we had put together her new little bed, with its shiny, red enameled frame. We were careful to allow a full six months between the older child's moving out of the crib and the younger's moving in, careful that she never felt that she was forced to pass her bed directly along to another baby, but still Sarah wept when its polished wood head and foot and sides were carried from the room.

Walker, for whom a crib was never better than an inadequately disguised cage, clapped at its second dismantling. He bounced on his version of the little bed, the same as his sister's but enameled in blue.

Between the two little beds is the fireplace, whose flue is permanently shut, bricked up. The empty hearth has become a cubbyhole for an appropriately combustible-looking collection of junked toys: Barbie's broken refrigerator and her hot-pink range, a fire engine without its wheels, stray blocks, twisted and retwisted pipe cleaners, ravaged coloring books—all trash they cannot bear to discard. Together the objects make a blaze and jumble of color. Presiding disconsolately over the heap is the piñata from the most recent birthday party. A papier-mâché donkey with a festive hide and mane of orange and red and pink tissue paper, he was torn in two, vivisected by preschool greed wielding a broom. Now his head and tail both face out into the bedroom, so we are spared the dispiriting sight of his hollow middle. The mantelpiece above bears another rubble of objects, most of which our daughter hopes to keep out of her brother's reach: stickers, costume jewelry, a collection of tiny plastic horses.

Propped in the center of the mantel is an old wall hanging: a wood bas-relief of a tavern, including kitchen, dining hall, and second-story bedrooms. Every object and gesture is carved and painted with cunning attention: dinner plates the size of dimes, a butter churn with a three-inch dash, washtubs, rolling pin, crucifix, table and benches, a clock whose hands read a quarter past five, hats hanging on hooks by the door, an accordion, two flowerpots, shotgun, and stove. My grandfather, who was apprenticed in 1904 to a cabinetmaker in Berlin (he was fourteen), acquired the hanging, which was made in the Black Forest. It used to contain a working music box, and just under the eaves is a brass key that no longer turns. The hidden mechanism, with its rolling, metal-toothed platen and minuscule comb of tines, once played, my grandfather told me, a feeble polka.

As a child, I spent many hours staring at the tavern's tiny furnishings, at once seduced and bewildered by the very nature of bas-relief, neither flat picture nor free sculpture, a dollhouse enduring an uneasy metamorphosis from three dimensions to two. Before we had children, I moved the tavern from closet to basement to guest room and back to closet, never knowing what to do with it until our children showed me.

"Take it down! I want to look at it up close!" one of them will say. The request is never more avid than when the children are ill, and I can remember exactly how fever enhanced the little row of frying pans hung over the stove, gilded the flowers painted on cupboard doors the size of my thumbnail. I can remember, in the glaze and glitter of their feverish eyes, but I can no longer *feel* the luxury of benign childhood illness, of recoveries uncompromised by meetings, deadlines, chores.

From experience, I know that if my children are not sufficiently entertained they will escape the confines of bed, and I supply toys, rescind the TV laws, and bring them from their room into ours. In our family, sick children inevitably end up in the parental bed, an indulgence intended to compensate for an ailment serious enough to mandate bed rest: a way of separating horizontal day from night, a chance to command the empire of our tall, king-size bed, at whose foot I prop the tavern.

"Why," Walker asks, as I asked my grandfather, "are the flames right on the pot?" A tiny black kettle hangs in the kitchen over kindling the size of matchsticks, its underside painted with tongues of red and yellow and orange.

"Because," I say, not finishing the answer any more than my grandfather did—in 1904 they didn't have cellophane for fake fires.

Not only my own childhood is recapitulated in our children's bedroom; their father's is here as well. Along the top shelf of the bookcase are twenty-nine bottles and nine glass inkwells, anywhere from ninety to a hundred and twenty years old. Clear, clouded, blue, green, amber—old enough so that none are actually colorless, so that even plain glass has acquired a purple tint. Though they were dug from old dumps, none are chipped or broken. There are hundreds of these bottles in our house, most packed away, all of them together representing thousands of hours of my husband's childhood, countless afternoons spent on his knees, alone or with a friend, excavating the past.

Time continues to possess and confound and mystify us. It passes, of course, with a relentlessness familiar to all grown-ups, but never more than when compared to the clock of childhood, with its burden of hours to be wasted, a burden compounded by the as yet misperceived vagaries of hour hands and minute hands and calendars. Questions of measurement include: When will it be Christmas, summer, Friday, my birthday? Dinner? Young children float on an ocean unmarked by adult dates and appointments. Sarah stands at the front door, dressed to go, whole hours before a birthday party. Walker looks out the window of the car, uttering "Are we there yet?" while still in our neighborhood.

He cannot imagine that his parents treasure long car rides for their enforced enclosure, their near-idleness.

But childhood has many hours that must be filled. Is this one reason for our curiously misguided idealization of it? Waiting for important phone calls, we read professional journals while riding our exercise bikes. Dinner cooks slowly in the Crock-Pot while I fold the laundry, catch the lead stories of the six-thirty news, and police the crayon situation (she takes his reds, he breaks her blues). How different from the time when we drooped over banisters, loitered limply at the back door, moaned, "But I have nothing to do. I'm so, so, so bored."

While our children wait to be older, imagining perhaps that grown-up busyness is a measure of happiness and freedom, they are amused by Barbies and blocks and crayons and tiny cars, by trains, stuffed animals, picture books, dress-up clothes, beads, stencils, pipe cleaners, fire engines, balls, balloons, putty, puzzles, and puppets. All of these, in every state of disrepair (Madison Avenue Barbie reduced to a gruesome paraplegic, her hair matted into dreadlocks), form a tide that washes over the surfaces of their room. Beds, tables, chairs—nothing is uncovered, clutter is fierce, the room infrequently tidy. Still, "What a great room!" people say when they enter for the first time. The walls are decorated with Babar and Mickey Mouse and Beatrix Potter, in determined contrast to my own room as a child, with its one print, entitled *In Disgrace,* of a little girl, face to the wall, blue sash drooping, socks rumpled, sad-eyed puppy at her scuffed heels. Flanking this print were two framed prayers by Mary Baker Eddy, the founder of Christian Science. Of a troubling and final nature, each seemed to indicate that I was not long for this world.

As a small child, I was high-spirited, careless, clumsy, and often in "Coventry," my British grandparents' way of saying "the doghouse." Even without the solace of canine sympathy, I knew myself to be that painted, rumple-socked girl sprung to life. Who needed to tell me that I was my mother's disgrace? She was pregnant and unmarried the summer after she graduated from high school, and every look she gave me was one of regret. My mother's parents reared me to be all that she was not—responsible and studious and steady—and they decorated my childhood bedroom to exclude the whimsy revealed in photographs of my mother's room, with its three dollhouses and trunks of dress-up clothes. Before I could read, I had a desk, a bookcase, and edifying messages on the wall—none of which helped to keep me out of the trouble I was bound to find.

Our daughter was still in the crib when I bought the giant Mickey Mouse decal, cut him out of the vast sheet of adhesive-backed vinyl, cut out each one of the rain of yellow stars that falls around him, placed them all with care as she watched from behind the polished bars of her crib. By design, the room is filled with happy nonsense, and yet Sarah seems already the studious child I was meant to be. "I'm going to my office," she says of her own art desk, a red-and-yellow-and-blue-and-green one, whose surface includes a light box for tracing. Sometimes she traces pictures, more often words, sentences. Her long hair falls around her while she works, hunched over in concentration, the light under her carefully moving pencil shining out through the dark strands.

"What are you doing?" I ask.

"My work," she says.

We redress the hurts of our own childhoods; we do it even with abundant evidence that our efforts rarely matter. Last Christmas, in the guise of Santa Claus, I bought Walker an inflatable clown. Three feet tall and weighted with sand at his feet, he is the type of long-suffering companion who, when hit, pops back up. Having struggled under the seen-and-not-heard rule that hopes to cure little girls of untoward zest, I found the clown irresistible. But the only time our little boy pushes him over is to use him as an inflatable log, a kind of bench. "What's the matter with him?" he asks me. "He won't lie down."

"Here," I say. "If you hit him, he pops up again." I demonstrate. Walker gives the clown a casual smack, shrugs. Every once in a while, passing through the children's room, I push the clown over, watch him rise cheerfully, inviting another assault.

I find that I come into the children's room when I am alone, anxious. Sarah and Walker are in school, the house is quiet. I put off work to sit in the chaise or lie on one of the beds that are so short I must curl, knees drawn up, to fit. Sometimes I tidy the room. If I can locate all the pieces of a board game, find both the left and the right of Barbie's pair of pink plastic pumps, my worries are somehow lessened by imposing order on chaos—even this happy chaos—by my ability to find something we assumed was lost. I especially like to complete the puzzles, whose pieces are always scattered. Colin's mother gave each of the children a wooden one, featuring a child of his or her own gender standing undressed before a closet. The little boy has interchangeable trousers and shirts and pairs of shoes, seven of each, and the little girl can try on skirts, jackets, dresses, and shoes.

For many months, the red cowboy boots have been missing from among the puzzle girl's accessories. One morning, I find the piece lodged under a baseboard in our room and feel a tiny leap of joy: the redemption of recovery. I go to put the piece away, so eager to press it into the empty boot-shaped space that as I cross the threshold from our room to the children's I almost miss what I am walking over. At my feet is a life-size version of the puzzle I am hoping to complete.

At five, our daughter is just beginning to understand herself as a creature of infinite possibility. We, her parents, each year let go of things we will likely never do, another trip we may not make, another sport we're too old to take up. But Sarah is just learning of her choices, all of which she relishes, lingers over. She asks to be wakened early enough to consider every option of what to wear to school, and on the floor of the room she lays out possible outfits: shoes, tights, dresses, pants, shirts, socks. She does it for herself and for her little brother, and, after they are dressed in the outfits they have picked, and are gone, the rejected clothes remain.

The room I see is this: their sleeping selves are laid out, pajamas on his bed, nightgown on hers. Among table legs, train tracks, and Barbie gear, his blue trousers and race-car shirt pose solemnly. The shirt's long sleeve reaches toward that of his sister's pink pullover, carefully tucked into the waist of a black skirt decorated all over with pink flowers. A second-choice skirt—she prefers the longer, purple one—it floats above the legs of red tights, legs splayed crazily as if in flight from this room, as if to remind us, and the attentive boy evoked by the posture of those empty dark blue trousers, that she is leaping forward into life. Soon she will not live in the bedroom next to ours. Soon she and her brother will have separate rooms, later separate homes and separate lives. This room will, perhaps, become the library we once planned, the chaise re-covered in a sober leather or corduroy.

But for now the children are here, in this room next to ours, his bed only nine steps from the one in which we sleep, hers fourteen. I measure these steps, walk them like a prayer.

How mysterious to have arrived in this place, this family, a child who never played house, who never held a doll, who never, not once, imagined herself a mother. How did it happen? From the shelf the puzzle girl returns my stare, her closet complete, her serenely smiling face as enigmatic—as exotic and unexpected—as a totem's.

HOME FOR THE
HOLIDAYS

Long after my friends and schoolmates had outgrown Santa Claus, I still believed in him. It was a secret, potentially embarrassing faith, one encouraged by my grandparents, who believed that, in other ways, I'd been forced to grow up too quickly. My parents' marriage ended when I was six months old, in 1961, in a community where divorce was still more scandal than commonplace. My mother's mother and father raised me in the house where she herself had been raised and where she lived until I was six. As I grew up, I saw my father only twice, and my mother's leaving was something I precipitated, unwittingly, one Christmas morning.

I'd woken up too early. Hours before dawn, I crept down the hall to the fireplace to see if my stocking had been filled. Outside, the winter sky was still black; wind rattled the windows in their frames. The stocking was heavy, stuffed with promise. Having touched it, I found I couldn't let go, and I lifted it from the nail and carried it to my mother's bedroom, next door to my own. Her room was utterly quiet; there was no sound of her breathing. Her bed, when I felt it, was cool, flat, empty.

Filled with dread—where could she be in the dark, wide night?—I went to my grandparents and woke them up.

"Mommy's not here," I said. "Mommy's gone."

As soon as my grandmother turned on the light, as soon as I saw her face, I knew that I had made a mistake. I hadn't saved my mother from whatever I was afraid might have befallen her. Instead, I had betrayed her.

She returned at seven, slipping through the kitchen door, her white Christmas Eve dress looking rumpled and dingy in the gray light of morning. The ensuing fight was spectacular, even for old enemies like my mother and grandmother. Loud enough to be heard through two sets of closed doors, it featured words I didn't know, words that rang with complex menace. *Assignation. Promiscuity.*

Each Christmas Eve, after I was asleep, my grandfather would take off his shoes and dip them in the ashes left from the fire. He carefully made footprints that led from the hearth across the beige carpet to the tree and back, then wiped the soles clean. He ate the cookies I'd set out on Santa's plate, shook crumbs on the tabletop, crumpled the napkin, drank the cold cocoa. In the morning, I noted all these signs and believed in them.

My stocking brimmed with gifts wrapped meticulously in marbled Florentine paper tied with narrow ribbons. I opened them slowly, with unnatural, unchildlike care. Inside were tiny carved bears, sets of colored pencils too small to sharpen, books the size of postage stamps. Always, the guiding aesthetic was of a life made as small as possible: an electric lamp complete with three-volt bulbs the size of apple seeds. It didn't matter that I had no dollhouse to plug it into. I didn't want, ever, to test it.

Adults find it difficult to reconcile the simultaneous knowing and unknowing that is inherent in faith. Children rarely try. I had many opportunities, even invitations, to conclude that it was my mother who filled my stocking. And I was old enough to have heard for years the playground challenge: *You don't believe in Santa, do you?* Well, no, I didn't, and yes, I did. What I believed in was some thing I identified as Santa Claus, having no more sophisticated language to articulate what I now understand as a longing for the ideal home. To me, this platonic space was so far away that it appeared as small as a dollhouse, but it was the place where my mother and I would someday live: a home too small and controlled to contain quarrels or tears.

The Christmas I was nine, my dark-haired, white-skinned mother went to Jamaica with a man I didn't know and came home on New Year's Day, her hair streaked blond, her white skin brown and peeling. In her absence, for which she tried to apologize with brightly painted maracas and pink shell bracelets, my grandmother had filled my stocking. On Christmas morning I saw right away that something was wrong. It was too lumpy, the things it contained too big: hair bands and candy, perfume, a matching pen and pencil set— nothing I wanted.

"How was Christmas?" my mother asked, sitting on the couch, scratching her sunburned arms. "What did Santa bring you?"

"Who?" I said disdainfully. *"Santa?* Why would I believe in something as stupid as Santa?"

The surprise and hurt on her face and on my grand-mother's was what I wanted, and yet I felt their quick intake of breath as if it were my own. I felt the air leave the room as if I'd struck the house itself, punishing it for being what it was, outsized and filled with mistakes lit by the glare of hundred-watt bulbs.

Now I live in the big city of New York, and my children are subjected each holiday season to a barrage of Santas—Santas ringing bells and asking for money, Santas sitting in depart-ment stores and posing for pictures, Santas doing the cancan in sync with the Rockettes. At five and seven, already they exchanged knowing looks with each other, having, I think, decided to spare me the truth.

So much of the holiday ritual—exhausting, essential—is about creating perfect moments, picturesque gatherings that cannot be sustained longer than a night, if that long. Years after the deaths of my mother and grandparents, I'm the stocking stuffer of the family, the one who travels hours to a store that sells small-scale horses with real horsehair manes and tails. I keep a bag hidden in a closet in my study and fill it with things I know my children will love. As early as June I am gathering little toys, things I won't allow myself to give them until the occasion—Christmas—presents the excuse I need. I can't face their father's accusations: *You spoil them. You buy them too much.*

And more damning: *These things aren't for them, they're for you. They're for a little girl who doesn't exist anymore.*

Except that she does, of course. We're all burdened by ourselves. This is what makes the holidays the celebrated trial we bemoan. There are so many hopes and longings, so many pasts and futures, all jostling and confused, that the

present can seem as thin and flimsy as the discarded wrap-
pings scattered around the tree. Just at that point when we're
confronted by the remains of it all, we find ourselves asking,
Was it worth it? Did it work? Were we all as happy together
as we thought?

INTERIOR CASTLES

I

"Forty coolies!" was my grandmother's abbreviated reference to her life in Shanghai a hundred years ago. She and her sister were cared for on an estate in the city's International Settlement. My grandmother would shake her head as she spoke the words "forty coolies," spoke them with wonder, not embarrassment. At the turn of the last century, Shanghai was home to many Europeans, expatriates who created their own little Englands and Germanys and Frances and whose households were served by Chinese labor that was unimaginably affordable. To illustrate, my grandmother would tell this story: One day an old groundskeeper fell from the top of the ladder while pruning a tree on the family's property. As he fell, he grabbed for the ladder and pulled it over with him. The head gardener came running from the greenhouse, picked up the ladder, dusted it off, and left the groundskeeper where he had fallen. When asked by my great-grandfather why he would pick up the ladder and not the man, the head gardener shrugged as if the answer were obvious. "Man old, ladder new," he said, and he bowed and returned to the greenhouse. In China, life was cheap, and, my grandmother would have added, dirty.

"The filth! The filth!" was the second most frequent of her invocations of the country in which she lived until she was seventeen. In an age without vaccines or antibiotics, where yellow fever and cholera and typhus outbreaks were common, dirt meant danger. From my grandmother's childhood home, "night soil" was collected by one of the under coolies (out of forty, one was designated for the literal shit work) and carried out to the street in the morning to be collected by an ox-drawn wagon when it passed on the boulevard. These wagons, called *kongs,* took human excrement to the rice paddies, where it was used as fertilizer, guaranteeing the contamination of waterways and the spread of cholera. My grandmother's only brother died before his second birthday, and according to family lore, what he died of was dirt. The little boy's death began before the meningitis subsequent to a teething infection; it began with his very birth in China. Even as the only son of an otherwise Orthodox Jewish family, he died uncircumcised because my grandmother's mother once saw black crescents of dirt under the Shanghai rabbi's long fingernails and was so frightened by the sight of them that she decided to wait until she could take her son home to a rabbi in London.

Seventy years later, if you were to put a plate of Chinese food before my grandmother, she would vomit. Traveling with me through New York City's Chinatown in the back of a taxi, she covered her eyes. And if she didn't readily offer her hand in greeting to an Asian person, it wasn't racism or snobbery (not exactly, although my grandmother was an imperious woman who never questioned her right to any of her wealth or possessions), but a fear of contagion that never diminished. Her family bought ivories and porcelains, silk rugs, jade, cloisonné; they decorated their homes in Shang-hai, and later in Nice, in London, and in Los Angeles, with these things. But that was the extent of their interaction with China. Much of the food they consumed was imported from England. Even the cows and the chickens were brought to them over the oceans—a long journey for livestock. "Orp-ingtons," my grandmother said the chickens were called. She spoke this name with rapture. "White and beautiful!" she said. What she meant, I knew, was *white and clean*.

Vegetables were grown on the family's own land and, be-fore they were eaten, scrubbed with carbolic soap, a poison-ous antiseptic detergent made from coal tar. Decades later, when washing anything she considered particularly dirty, my grandmother would whisper the words "carbolic soap" to herself and would shake her head with longing. Clearly, nothing could be dependably laundered without it. For me, a child born in Los Angeles in 1961, the words had a quaintly ridiculous ring, and yet one winter, when our children suc-cumbed to a particularly virulent and tenacious stomach virus, I found myself collapsed, despairing, over our washer. If only I had carbolic soap, I knew the germs would perish.

In Shanghai, my grandmother remembered, she once glanced through the open door of a hotel kitchen and saw a Chinese pastry chef patting a pie crust flat on his bare, sweat-ing belly—despite the incontrovertible "fact," my grand-mother assured me, that Chinese people bathed only once a year. Her own ritual of hygiene, to which I listened from outside her tightly closed bathroom door, included such vig-orously loud scrubbing and frantic splashing that it sounded as if she were trying to lather up a tiger rather than her own assumably cooperative limbs.

Every day that she lived in China, my grandmother learned that a home was maintained in opposition to the world around it. That was the kind of home she made in Los

Angeles; that was the home in which I grew up. When she married another displaced British subject, a man whose mild personality was eclipsed by her fierceness, she made a life with him that confined rather than supported and that invited rebellion from my American-born mother. In an inspired flight of defiance, my mother found my father, who was raised in El Paso, Texas, and who had a Baptist preacher for one grandfather and a Methodist for the other. My parents were as ill suited to each other as might be imagined, and their marriage was short-lived. When it was over, my mother gave me to her mother as the replacement daughter she believed would buy her freedom. At least that was her version of the story. "You were supposed to ransom me," she explained.

Since the same woman raised us, mine was not the typical Los Angeles childhood any more than my mother's had been. My grandmother emphatically disapproved of all things American and encouraged me to form myself in contrast to the children around me. American children stayed up too late, talked back, ate what and when they pleased, accompanied their parents to adult social functions, wore vulgar clothing, watched too much television, chewed gum, went to bed with wet hair, slouched at table, slacked off on schoolwork, etc. All of this was the fault of their permissive parents.

What patience my grandmother had was elicited only by surrender. Because she had great reserves of tenderness for orphans and strays, both human and animal, I suspect she loved me all the more for having effected my abandonment. At the time of my birth, my parents were eighteen and had been married for six months. As soon as my mother brought me home from the hospital, my grandmother hired a baby nurse, engaged a diaper service, and launched a campaign to oust my father. My father himself planned to be a preacher, and a preacher, she argued, would never be able to support my mother in the style to which she was accustomed. Furthermore, if they remained together, she'd cut my mother off without a penny.

Having raised a spoiled, dependent daughter, my grandmother knew the threats to frighten her: no pretty clothes or picture hats; no ironed pillow slips; no chaise longue in the shade of the jacaranda; no tray of cool drinks perspiring on the patio. She exhorted my grandfather to forget that he'd once been a poor boy and scripted the farewell speech for him to deliver.

Perhaps it was easier to kick my father out of the garden than out of the house; my grandfather led him outside, among the tangerine and lemon trees. "Go back home," he told him, and he released my father from the burden of child support, and from the privilege of visiting me.

Even if I didn't articulate it to myself, I recognized danger at the hands of someone so potentially ruthless as my grandmother. I eavesdropped on my mother's fights with her mother and, afraid that someday I, too, might fall from grace, I ended by making myself my grandmother's servant: safe by virtue of being useful. But that was later. First I was her pet, and her audience.

"Tell me a story," I'd beg. "Please!" The world my grandmother created was so expansive and exotic that as a young child I didn't, like my mother, feel imprisoned in her home. Nana's memories of Shanghai were vivid, and her youth had included such adventures as traveling from Harbin, China, to Paris on the Orient Express. She'd married late, at forty-two, in Las Vegas. But I didn't want to hear about that, the wedding that went off, small and seemingly incidental as compared to the ones that did not.

"Tell me about the dress!"

"What do you want to hear about that for?" my grandmother would say. But her protests were perfunctory. She liked to tell stories of how she had spurned suitors.

"Well," she relented, smiling, "as you know, the dress was the worst of it." She always began with her most memorable transgression, the engagement she broke when she didn't show up at the altar. "The dress and the gifts." She set the teapot on the table and sat down next to me on the sprung sofa.

If I closed my eyes I could see my grandmother as a young woman, her hair falling dark and heavy down the back of the white gown. I pictured her alone on a wide avenue, triumphant and huge in her wedding dress, as big as a parade float and moving determinedly away from the synagogue that held the expectant groom and congregation.

I can't remember the would-be husband's name, but I know all about the gown. It had a six-foot train and was made to order by Lanvin, in Paris. Along with my grandmother's entire trousseau, it was packed in layers of tissue paper and shipped to Shanghai.

"What happened to it?" I asked.

"They auctioned it off at a benefit for the fever hospital. Or maybe it was smallpox. Something dreadful." She couldn't, after all, return a couture wedding dress. "I did keep the underclothes," she said, sighing with pleasure at the thought of them. The lace on her lingerie was made by nuns. Handwork of virgins, it adorned knickers, brassieres, chemises, and negligees: everything as white as cake icing, ready to be stripped away on the wedding night.

Born in 1899, my grandmother grew up in a society that arranged its marriages. Most young women accepted this as inevitable, but she never made peace with the custom. When she tried to comply, her efforts were short-lived, the results disastrous.

Gifts for weddings that didn't take place had to be returned, of course, each with a letter of apology. I asked my grandmother what she wrote in those long-ago letters, how she explained that instance of what was, she led me to believe, a habit.

She shrugged. "Sorry, I suppose. I told them I was sorry."

How many men did my grandmother jilt? Her first engagement was to Lawrence (later Lord) Kadoorie, with whom she had played as a child. Their fathers were business partners, and their families neighbors in Shanghai's International Settlement. It was assumed my grandmother would marry Lawrence, but she escaped that betrothal before a wedding date could be set.

"You did like him," I'd prompt.

"Yes," she conceded.

"So what happened?"

She shrugged and sighed and shook her head. "We went out to dinner and he added up the bill on his sleeve. Lawrence Kadoorie, with all his millions, used a pencil on his shirt cuff to check the addition. He licked its tip and bent his head over his wrist and I thought, Well, I won't spend my life with a man like that."

When Lord Kadoorie died a few years ago, his obituary in *The New York Times* was of a length befitting a billionaire philanthropist, but my grandmother, who knew of the steady rise of his fortunes, never expressed any regret at not being the wife of a man of fabulous, fairy-tale wealth. Unless I asked her to tell the story of the shirt cuff, she spoke of Lawrence only as a boy, and most often her memory returned to one afternoon during the monsoon season, when they had run together over the windy, wet lawns, each pursued by a scolding governess.

I have a photograph of my grandmother at seventeen, the age at which she was promised to Lawrence. She smolders in the portrait. Against her smooth throat lies a string of pearls her father gave her, one that I inherited. My grandmother wore that necklace every day of her life. She took it off to bathe and then put it back on again.

"Why do you wear your pearls to the market?" I asked her once.

"You have to wear pearls every day," she said. "They have to be against your skin." She touched them. Now that she was old and thin, they hung lower than they had in the portrait. "If you don't wear pearls," she said, "they die. They go gray and dull."

It sounded fanciful, but maybe my grandmother was right. I haven't worn the pearls, and recently I discovered that the white luster of a few of the larger ones has vanished. I think, though, that the reason my grandmother guarded the necklace so literally close to her heart was that it was a gift from her father, who loved her extravagantly and whose love she returned in like measure. Was it because she felt no other man lived up to the father she adored that my grandmother didn't marry until after he died? She thwarted him, though. She rejected every match he made for her, and she did it flagrantly. "Poor Rube," she'd say. "Poor David." She'd shake her head, but I could tell that the gesture was one of manufactured sympathy, a tenderness she'd been taught to express.

The year after the wedding dress was sold—its seams perhaps opened and resewn to fit another bride—my grandmother's father took her to California. He bought her a chestnut horse on whose back she liked to gallop through the orange groves of Pasadena, and he managed to secure an invitation for her to ride that horse in the 1919 Rose Parade. My grandmother reported such indulgences with a relish undiminished by time. Now, years later, I find myself wondering if perhaps my great-grandfather loved his daughter too jealously. Did he offer her husbands he knew she'd refuse?

"I didn't want a husband, I guess," she'd say, shrugging.

"But you married Bop," I said.

"Because I did want a baby."

In 1942, three years after her father's death, my grandmother might have been sufficiently modern to consider single motherhood, but she knew that society would still penalize a fatherless child, so she married. She chose her husband for his meekness, and she kept all her inheritance separate from my grandfather's money.

"I have one piece of advice for you," she said when I told her of my own marriage plans. We were standing in her kitchen, and she crossed her arms and then backed me into the corner between stove and sink.

"What's that?" I said.

"Separate bank accounts."

"Oh come on," I said.

"Be sensible!" she said. "Not romantic. What if you want to leave him? What if you want to clear out in a hurry?"

In love, some people do tend to leave, while the rest of us get left.

"I guess now it's four of them," my daughter said to me after school one day. She fell back on the sofa and sighed gustily. The four were Drew, Jack, Kevin, and Dylan. I chaperoned a play date with Dylan. When Sarah stubbed her toe, he fell on the floor at her feet.

"Please," he begged, "let me make it better." He reached for her pant leg, his eyes hot with new love. "I know a secret way."

"I don't think so." Sarah withdrew her foot from his eager hands. She was sitting in the same chair in which my grandmother had first held her.

Nana was ninety-one when my daughter was born. She was crooked and gnarled and irascible, and as she bent whispering over the baby, I saw the dangerous old fairy from childhood tales, the one whom wise parents are careful not to slight. I couldn't hear what she was saying to her only great-granddaughter, but I know what wish my grandmother would have bestowed, and I know my daughter.

"You'll break their hearts," she must have said.

Break their hearts, and avenge her humiliation. More than sixty years had passed, but still, she was stinging. In Nice, France, in 1925, having exhausted her father's offerings, my grandmother found, or was found by, a prince. Titled and penniless, the handsome White Russian was after her money; of this my great-grandparents were sure. Forbidden to see him, threatened with the same punishment she would use to bully my mother—if she disobeyed, if she married him, she would lose her inheritance—at night my grandmother slipped away from the family villa to meet her Russian lover. The chauffeur tried to blackmail her; the butler lectured her on fallen women; her sister provided the distraction of a different scandal, that of a lesbian affair. My grandmother promised the Russian that she loved him enough to live as a pauper, and he left her. Her parents had been right; that wasn't what he'd had in mind.

What was his name? What was his name? What was his name? I knew that eventually I would wear her down. She'd tell me if only to get me to stop.

"Michael Evlanoff. I was a fool, and my father was right. He came to this country a few years after I did. Married Elizabeth Arden, and then she divorced him." My grandmother looked at me across the breakfast table. "That's all I have to say," she said, and she laid her knife on the edge of her plate.

Armed with these few facts, after my grandmother's death, I went to the public library to find out what I could, an obituary, a photograph. I wanted to know what he looked like, this alleged prince who had, unwittingly, changed my mother's life, and my own.

According to the 1957 edition of *Current Biography,* on December 30, 1942, Elizabeth Arden married "Russian-born Prince Michael Evlanoff, a naturalized American citizen, from whom she obtained an uncontested divorce in 1944." The wedding announcement in *The New York Times* called Evlanoff a "member of a prominent family of the former Russian nobility . . . son of the late Prince Basil Evlanoff, and the late Princess Evlanoff . . . of a family dating back to the tartar warlords of the twelfth century."

"After the Russian Revolution," the announcement continued, "he made his home in Paris . . . Recently he had been residing at the Sherry-Netherland."

There was an obituary as well, from May 9, 1972: "Michael Evlanoff, who wrote a biography of Alfred Nobel, died yesterday in the Florence Nightingale Nursing Home. He was 76 years old. Mr. Evlanoff, descended from Tartar princes, graduated from the Russian Artillery School and served in World War I. His book, 'Nobel-Prize Donor; Inventor of Dynamite—Advocate of Peace,' was published in 1944. His marriage in 1942 to Mrs. Elizabeth Graham Lewis, founder of Elizabeth Arden, Inc., the cosmetics company, ended in divorce."

I found his biography of Alfred Nobel, published by the Blakiston Company and dedicated to "My darling mother and Emmanuel Nobel, who were the guiding stars in my life." A romantic and melancholy work, characterized by a longing for what has been lost forever, it told me that Evlanoff met Emmanuel Nobel, the nephew of Alfred, in 1919, when both served in the Great War. The two men met in the Caucasus, "that beautiful and precious pearl of Russia." I paged through the portraits of the Nobels, hoping one of the photographs might include the author, but none did. And, as the dust jacket was missing, I was left with a vague and generic picture of an old man in pajamas, bewildered by my visit to the nursing home in Manhattan.

"Margaret Esme Sassoon Benjamin," I would repeat her name to him until it produced a response. "You do remember her, don't you?"

My imagined Prince Evlanoff had a day's worth of gray stubble on his chin and a handkerchief tucked into the breast pocket of his pajama top. He seemed confused by my interrogation.

Would the real Evlanoff have remembered my grandmother, a woman whom he had not embraced for nearly fifty years? The question depended on how long and how serious their affair had been.

Through connections provided by a cousin in Paris, I wrote to an elderly White Russian, one who had also lived in Nice during the twenties. Did he know anything of a Michael Evlanoff, possibly Ivlanov, when the prince lived in France? I was researching my grandmother's past, I explained.

The answer, from this gentleman who was a member of the Union of Russian Nobility in Paris, was prompt. No

Evlanoff or Ivlanov ever existed in the official records of the Nobility of the Russian Empire; the name was entirely unknown. He was sorry to be the bearer of such news. In Nice, when he was a young student, he had himself had the misfortune of meeting certain Russians who pretended nobility for social or material gain. This pained him, he wrote, and it was a blow to what he called his national pride, but, alas, it was the unpleasant truth, and he was honor bound to tell me so.

SEEKING RAPTURE

My mother died of breast cancer when I was twenty-four. I took care of her while she died. I gave her her morphine, her Halcion, her Darvocet, Percocet, Demerol, Zantac, and prednisone. I bathed her and I dressed her bedsores. Though I had to force myself into such communion with disease, I kissed her each morning when she woke and each evening as she fell asleep. Then I went into the bathroom, took a cotton pad soaked with rubbing alcohol, and scrubbed my lips until they burned and bled. Sometimes as I did this I thought of Saint Catherine of Siena, who in 1373 collected into a bowl the pus from the open breast-cancer lesions of Andrea, an older member of the Mantellate lay order to which Catherine belonged. Andrea had caused Catherine much trouble and public censure some years before when she had implied that the saint's infamous raptures and fasts were a pretense rather than a manifestation of holiness. The bowl's foul contents stank and made Catherine retch, but both in penance for her disgust and in determination to love her enemy,

Catherine drank the old nun's pus. That night Catherine had a vision of Christ. Her holy bridegroom bade her to His side, and she drank the blood of life that flowed from His wounds.

"You were named for saints and queens," my mother told me when I was young enough that a halo and a crown seemed interchangeable. We were not Catholics yet. Judaism was our birthright, but we had strayed early, and now we were members of the Twenty-eighth Church of Christ, Scientist. Each Sunday, we drove together to the bland, beige sanctuary on Hilgard Avenue in West Los Angeles, where she attended church while I, in a lesser building, went to Sunday school. Above my bed was a plaque bearing these words from the church's founder, Mary Baker Eddy: "Father-Mother good, lovingly Thee I seek, Patient, meek. In the way Thou hast, Be it slow or fast, Up to Thee." The little prayer, which I was taught to recite as I fell asleep, worried me. I did not want to die fast. I had asthma, and each attack seemed capable of killing me, so when I was not thinking of my mother, whom I loved without measure, I thought of death and of God. They made my first trinity: Mother, Death, God.

I might have remained immune to the mind-over-matter doctrines of Mrs. Eddy and to the subsequent seduction of the saints had I not, when I was six, suffered an accident that occasioned a visit to a Christian Science "practitioner," or healer. The circumstances were these: my mother, divorced when I was not yet a year old and when she was not yet nineteen, had recently moved out of her parents' house on Sunset Boulevard, a house where I continued to live, as an only child, with my grandparents. It was the first of my mother's attempts to make a separate life for herself—a life that did not seem possible to her unless motherhood were left behind—and so now it was my grandfather who drove me to school each day. Though I already knew that my birth had interrupted my mother's education, I now came to understand that my continued existence somehow distracted her from her paralegal job and, worse, chased off romantic prospects. Each time my mother undressed before me my eyes were drawn to the shiny, pink stretch marks that pregnancy had traced over her stomach; they seemed emblematic of the greater damage I had done. In the afternoons I sat in the closet of her old room, inhaling her perfume from what dresses remained; each morning I woke newly disappointed at the sight of her empty bed in the room next to mine. So, despite my grandfather's determined cheer, it was a glum ride to school that was interrupted, dramatically, the day the old Lincoln's brakes failed.

Pumping the useless pedal, my grandfather turned off the road in order to avoid rear-ending the car ahead of us. We went down a short embankment, picked up speed, crossed a ditch, and hit one of the stately eucalyptus trees that form the boundary between Sunset Boulevard and the UCLA campus. On impact, the glove compartment popped open; since I was not wearing my seat belt, I sailed forward and split my chin on its lock mechanism, cracking my jawbone.

My grandfather was not hurt. He got me out of the wrecked, smoking car and pressed a folded handkerchief to my face. Blood was pouring out of my mouth and chin, and I started to cry from fear more than pain. I was struggling against the makeshift compress when, by a strange coincidence, my mother, en route to work, saw us from the street and pulled over. Her sudden materialization, the way she sprang nimbly out of her blue car, seemed to me angelic, magical—an impression enhanced by the dress she was wearing that morning, which had a tight bodice and a full crimson skirt embroidered all over with music notes. Whenever she wore this dress I was unable to resist touching the fabric of the skirt. I found the notes evocative, mysterious; and if she let me I would trace my finger over the spiral of a treble clef or feel the stitched dots of the notes, as if they represented a different code from that of music, like Braille or Morse, a message that I might in time decipher.

My mother was unusually patient and gentle as she helped me into her car. We left my grandfather waiting for a tow truck and drove to UCLA's nearby medical center, where I was X-rayed and then prepared for suturing. I lay under a light so bright that it almost forced me to close my eyes, while a blue, disposable cloth with a hole cut out for my chin descended over my face like a shroud, blocking my view of my mother. I held her hand tightly, too tightly perhaps, because after a moment she pried my fingers off and laid my hand on the side of the gurney. She had to make a phone call, she said; she had to explain why she hadn't shown up at work.

I tried to be brave, but when I heard my mother's heels clicking away from me on the floor, I succumbed to an animal terror and tried to kick and claw my way after her. It took both the doctor and his nurse to restrain me. Once they had, I was tranquilized before I was stitched and then finally taken home asleep.

Later that afternoon I woke up screaming in a panic that had been interrupted, not assuaged, by the drug. My mother, soon exhausted by my relentless crying and clinging to her neck, her legs, her fingers—to whatever she would let me hold—took me to a practitioner whose name she picked at random from the Twenty-eighth Church of Christ, Scientist's directory.

The practitioner was a woman with gray hair and a woolly, nubbly sweater, which I touched as she prayed over me, my head in her lap and one of her hands on my forehead, the other over my heart. Under those hands, which I remember as cool and calm and sparing in their movements, I felt my fear drain away. Then the top of my skull seemed to be opened by a sudden, revelatory blow, and a searing light filled me. Mysteriously, unexpectedly, this stranger had ushered me into an experience of something I cannot help but call rapture. I felt myself separated from my flesh and from all earthly things. I felt myself no more corporeal than the tremble in the air over a fire. I had no words for what happened—I have few now, almost forty years later—and in astonishment I stopped crying. My mother sighed in relief, and I learned, at age six, that transcendence was possible: that spirit could conquer matter, and that therefore I could overcome whatever obstacles prevented my mother's loving me. I could overcome myself.

In the years following the accident I became increasingly determined to return to wherever it was I had visited in the practitioner's lap, and I thought the path to this place might be discovered in Sunday school. Around the wood laminate table I was the only child who had done the previous week's assignment, who had marked my white-vinyl-covered Bible with the special blue chalk pencil and had read the corresponding snippet from Mary Baker Eddy's *Science and Health with Key to the Scriptures*. The other children lolled and dozed in clip-on neckties and pastel-sashed dresses while I sat up straight. The teacher had barely finished asking a question before my hand, in its white cotton glove buttoned tight at the wrist, shot up. Sometimes I would see the teacher looking at me with what seemed, even then, like consternation. The lassitude of the other children, their carelessly incorrect answers that proceeded from lips still bearing traces of hastily consumed cold cereal, was clearly what she expected. What was disconcerting was my fierce recital of verses, my vigilant posture on the edge of the red plastic kindergarten chair.

The arena of faith was the only one in which I felt I had a chance of securing my mother's attention. Since she was not around during the week to answer to more grubby requirements, and since she was always someone who preferred the choice morsel, it was to my mother rather than to my grandparents that the guidance of my soul had been entrusted. On Sundays, after church, we went to a nearby patio restaurant, where we sat in curlicued wrought-iron chairs and reviewed my Sunday school lesson while eating club sandwiches held together with fancy toothpicks. The waiters flirted with my mother, and men at neighboring tables smiled in her direction. They looked at her left hand, which had no ring. They seemed to share my longing for my mother—who already embodied for me the beauty of youth, who had the shiny-haired, smooth-cheeked vitality my grandparents did not have, who could do backbends and cartwheels and owned high-heeled shoes in fifteen colors—who became ever more precious for her elusiveness.

I grew impatient with *Key to the Scriptures,* and in order to reexperience the ecstatic rise that had for an instant come through the experience of pain, I began secretly—and long before I had the example of any saint—to practice the mortification of my flesh. At my grandfather's workbench, I turned his vise on my finger joints. When my grandmother brought home ice cream from Baskin-Robbins and discarded the dry ice with which it was packed, I used salad tongs to retrieve the small, smoking slab from the trash can. In the privacy of the upstairs bathroom, I touched my tongue to the dry ice's surface and left a little of its skin there. I looked in the mirror at the blood coming out of my mouth, at the same magic flow that had once summoned my mother from the impossibly wide world of grown-ups and traffic and delivered her to my side.

My mother converted to Catholicism when I was ten, and I followed in her wake, seeking her even as she sought whatever it was that she had not found in Christian Science. We had failed at even the most basic of Mrs. Eddy's tenets, for by then we routinely sought the care of medical doctors. At first we went only for emergencies, like the accident to my chin, but then my mother developed an ulcer and I, never inoculated, got tetanus from a scrape—physical collapses stubbornly unaffected by our attempts to disbelieve in them.

In preparation for my first Communion, I was catechized by a priest named Father Dove. Despite this felicitous name, Father Dove was not the Holy Spirit incarnate: he chain-smoked and his face over his white collar had a worldly, sanguine hue. Worse, I suspected that my mother was in love with him. She fell in love easily. One Saturday I made my first confession (that I had been rude to my grandmother and had taken three dollars from her purse), and the next day I took Communion with eleven other little girls dressed in white; from that time forward I attended mass in a marble sanctuary filled with gilt angels.

Light came through the stained-glass windows and splashed colors over everything. A red circle fell on my mother's white throat. Incense roiled around us, and I looked down to compare the shiny toes of my black patent-leather shoes with those of hers. When we left, lining up to shake Father Dove's hand, I was able to study the faces around me and confirm that my mother's wide hazel eyes, her long nose, and high, white forehead made her more beautiful than anyone else.

For Christmas the following year I received, in my stocking, a boxed set of four volumes of *Lives of the Saints,* intended for children. There were two volumes of male saints, which I read once, flipping through the onionskin pages, and then left in my dresser drawer, and two of female saints, which I studied and slept with. The books contained color plates, illustrations adapted from works of the masters. Blinded Lucy. Maimed Agatha, her breasts on a platter. Beheaded Agnes. Margaret pressed to death under a door piled high with stones. Perpetua and Felicity mauled by beasts. Well-born Clare, barefoot and wearing rags. Mary Magdalen de' Pazzi lying on the bed of splinters she made for herself in the woodshed. Veronica washing the floors with her tongue, and Angela drinking water used to bathe a leper's sores. I saw that there were those who were tortured and those who needed no persecutors—they were enemies to their own flesh.

Saint Catherine of Siena began by saying Hail Marys on every step she climbed. Soon she slept on a board, with a brick for a pillow. She did not like her hair shirt because it smelled, so she took to wearing an iron chain that bit into her waist. As Catherine's *Dialogue* (dictated years later while she was in a sustained ecstasy that lasted weeks, even months) makes clear, she believed earthly suffering was the only way to correct the intrinsic baseness of mankind.

My mother also held forth an ideal of perfection, an ideal for which she would suffer, but hers was beauty. For beauty she endured the small tortures of eyebrow plucking and peel-off facial masks, of girdles and pinched toes, of sleep sacrificed to hair rollers and meals reduced to cottage cheese. I knew, from my mother's enthusiastic response to certain pictures in magazines and to particular waifs in the movies, that the child who would best complement her vanity was dark-haired and slender and balanced on point shoes. I was blond, robust, and, at thirteen, still given to tree climbing. Because my conception had been accidental, because I ought not to have been there at all, it must have struck my mother as an act of defiance that I was so large a child, taller and sturdier than any other girl in my class.

I wished myself smaller. I began to dream at night of Beyond the Looking Glass potions, little bottles bearing liquids that shrank me to nothing and mushrooms that let me disappear between grass blades. I began, too, to dread Sunday lunches with my mother, who fastidiously observed my fork in its ascension to my mouth.

Saint Catherine was fourteen when her older sister Bonaventura died in childbirth. Catherine blamed herself for her sister's death. She believed God had punished her and Bonaventura because Catherine had let her big sister tempt her into using cosmetics and curling her hair—because she had let Bonaventura's example convince her, briefly, that a woman could embrace both heavenly and earthly desires.

Whatever buoyancy, whatever youthful resilience, Saint Catherine had disappeared when she lost her sister. She became uncompromising in turning away from all worldly things: from food, from sleep, from men. Their mother, Lapa, a volatile woman whose choleric screams were reputedly so loud that they frightened passersby on Siena's Via dei Tintori, redoubled her efforts to marry her uncooperative twenty-fourth child. Some accounts hold that Catherine's intended groom was Bonaventura's widowed husband, a foul-tongued and occasionally brutish man. Catherine refused; she had long ago promised herself to Christ. She cut off her hair and fasted, eating only bread and uncooked vegetables. She began to experience ecstasies, and it is recorded that when she did she suffered a tetanic rigor in her limbs. Then

Lapa would lift her daughter from the floor where she had fallen and almost break the girl's bones as she tried to bend her stiff arms and legs.

Though it had been ten years since my mother moved out, she had yet to find a place that suited her for any length of time, and so she received her mail at the more permanent address of her parents and would stop by after work to pick it up. She came in the back door, cool and perfumed and impeccably dressed, and she drifted into the kitchen to find me in my rumpled school uniform, standing before the open refrigerator. One day I turned around with a cold chicken leg in my hand. My mother had tossed her unopened bills on the counter and was slowly rereading the message inside a greeting card decorated with a drawing of two lovesick rabbits locked in a dizzy embrace. She smiled slightly—a small and self-consciously mysterious smile—and kept the content of the card averted from my eyes. When she had had her fill of it, she looked up at me. She said nothing but let her eyes rest for a moment on the meat in my hand; then she looked away, from it, from me. She did not need to speak to tell me of her disapproval, and by now my habitual response to my mother had become one of despair: muffled, mute, and stumbling. But in that moment when she looked away from me, hopelessness gave way before a sudden, visionary elation. I dropped the drumstick into the garbage can. The mouthful I had swallowed stopped in its descent, and I felt it, gelid and vile inside me as I washed the sheen of grease from my fingers. At dinnertime, after my mother had left for her apartment, I pleaded too much homework to allow time to eat at the table, and I took my plate from the kitchen to my bedroom and opened the window, dropping the food into the dark foliage of the bushes below.

When I was fifteen my mother forsook the parish to which we belonged, and we began to attend one of the few Los Angeles churches that offered Latin mass. It was a romantic choice, I believe, one that justified for her the long and mostly silent drive we took each Sunday. During the celebration of the Eucharist, the priest would place the Communion wafer on my tongue. I withdrew it into my mouth carefully, making the sign of the cross over myself. Back in the pew I knelt and laid my head in my arms in a semblance of devotion, stuck out my tongue, and pushed the damp wafer into my sleeve. I was a little afraid of going to hell, very afraid of swallowing bread. My rules had grown more inexorable than the Church's; they alone could save me. But the Host was the Host, and I could not bring myself to throw it away. So I kept it in my sock drawer with my other relics: A small fetish of my mother's hair, stolen strand by strand from the hairbrush she kept in her purse. An eye pencil from that same source. Two tiny cookies from a Christmas stocking long past, a gingerbread boy and girl, no taller than an inch. A red leather collar from my cat, which had died.

I still had my little books of the female saints. I looked at them before bedtime some nights, stared at their little portraits, at bleeding hands and feet, at exultant faces tipped up to heaven. But I read longer hagiographies now, grown-up ones. When Catherine was twenty-four she experienced a mystical death. "My soul was loosed from the body for those four hours," she told her confessor, who recorded that her heart stopped beating for that long. Though she did not want to return to her flesh, Jesus bade her go back. But henceforth, she was not as other mortals; her flesh was changed and unfit for worldly living. From that time forward she swallowed nothing she did not vomit. Her happiness was so intense that she laughed in her fits of ecstasy; she wept and laughed at the same time.

I began to lose weight and watched with exultation as my bones emerged. I loved my transformed self. I could not look at myself enough, and I never went into the bathroom that I did not find myself helplessly undressing before the mirror. I touched myself, too. At night I lay in bed and felt each jutting rib, felt sternum and hipbone, felt my sharp jaw and with my finger traced the orbit of my eye. Like Catherine's, mine was not a happiness that others understood, for it was the joy of a private, inhuman triumph and of a universe— my body—utterly subjugated to my will.

My life was solitary, as befits a religious. Too much of human fellowship was dictated by taking meals in company, and what I did and did not consume separated me from others. Since I had not yet weaned myself completely from human needs, I drank coffee, tea, and Tab. I ate raw vegetables, multivitamins, NōDōz, and, when I felt very weak, tuna canned in water. When I climbed stairs I saw stars. I ate with my grandparents when I was forced to, but the mask of compliance was temporary, and upstairs, in my bathroom, I vomited what I had eaten. This will make you pure, I used to think when I made myself throw up. I used ipecac, the emetic kept in first-aid kits that causes a reeling, sweaty nausea that made me wish I were dead.

My grandmother and grandfather, sixty-two and seventy-one at my birth, were now old enough that their ebbing energy granted me freedom unusual for a teenager. Losing their sight, they did not see my thinness. Deaf, they never heard me in my bathroom. By the time I was sixteen and a licensed driver, they sometimes depended on me to buy groceries, and en route to the supermarket I would stop at the mall. "Where did you go, Kalamazoo?" my grandmother would ask when I returned, trying to understand why I was hours late. Sometimes she accused me of secretly meeting boys; she used the word *assignation*. But I had always spent my time alone. In the department stores I went from rack to rack, garment to garment: size two, size two, size two. Each like a rosary bead: another recitation, another confirmation of my size, one more turn of the key in the lock of safety.

Having conquered hunger, I began on sleep, and one night, in my room, very late, and in the delusional frenzy of having remained awake for nearly seventy-three hours, I began to weep with what I thought was joy. It seemed to me that I had almost gotten there: my flesh was almost utterly turned to spirit. Soon I would not be mortal; soon I would be as invulnerable as someone who could drink pus and see God.

The next day, however, I fainted and suffered a seizure that left me unable for a day to move the fingers on my right hand. In the same hospital where I had long ago attacked the ER nurse with my fingernails, I had an electroencephalogram and a number of other tests, which proved inconclusive. A different nurse, a different doctor, a different wing of the hospital. But nothing had changed: my mother was making a phone call in the corridor.

College gave me the opportunity to leave home, and I recovered partially. At heart, I wanted to believe in a different life, and I stopped going to mass and gained a little weight. I wore my mother's clothing, castoffs and whatever I could steal from her, articles that filled the reliquary of my peculiar faith. I zipped and buttoned myself into her garments as if they could cloak me with her love. Like miracle seekers who would tear hair, fingers—whatever they could—from a holy person's body, I was desperate, and one September I took my mother's favorite skirt from under the dry-cleaning bag hanging in the backseat of her car. It was purple, long, and narrow. I packed it in my suitcase and took it to school with me. She called me on the phone a week later. "Send it back," she said. I denied having taken it. "You're lying," she said.

I wore the skirt twice, and when it fell from the hanger I let it remain on the dark, dirty floor of my closet. When my mother called me again, I decided to return it, but there was a stain on the waistband that the dry cleaner could not remove. For an hour I sat on my dorm bed with the skirt in my lap, considering. Finally I washed it with Woolite and ruined it. I returned the skirt to my mother's closet when invited, during spring break, for dinner at her apartment. Please, I begged silently, tucking it between two other skirts. Please don't say anything more about it. Please. When she called me late that night at my grandparents' house, I hung up on her. Then I went into the bathroom, and I sat on the floor and wept.

At the end of her life, I waited for my mother to tell me how much she loved me and how good a daughter I had always been. I had faith that my mother was waiting until then to tell me that all along she had known I had performed impossible feats of self-alchemy.

After the funeral I packed up her apartment and looked through all her papers for a note, a letter left for me and sealed in an envelope. I closed my eyes and saw it: a meticulous, fountain-pen rendition of *Kathryn* on creamy stationery. When I didn't find that, I looked for clues to her affection. I read what correspondence she had saved. I reviewed check registers dating back ten years. I learned how much she had spent on dry cleaning her clothes, on her cats' flea baths, and on having her car radio repaired.

The death of my mother left me with a complex religious apparatus that now lacked its object, and I expected then to become an atheist. I frankly looked forward to the sterile sanity of it, to what relief it would bring. But I could not not believe. The habit of faith, though long focused misguidedly on a mortal object, persisted, and after a few years I found myself returning to the Church. Sporadically, helplessly, I attended mass. Having relearned to eat earthly food, now I practiced swallowing the Eucharist.

Rapture, too, returned. Long after I had stopped expecting it, it overcame me on a number of otherwise unnoteworthy occasions. I excused this as a fancy born of longing, as an endorphin effect brought on by exercise or pain, as craziness, pure and simple. But none of these described the experience, that same searing, light-filled, ecstatic rise, neither pleasant nor unpleasant, for no human measure applied to what I felt: transcendence. For the first time, I entrusted my spiritual evolution to some power outside my self and my will. If I was going to reach any new plane, any enlightenment, it would have to be God who transported me.

In the last months of her life, Catherine lost the use of her legs. Her biographers record that for years she had lived on little more than water and what sustenance she got from chewing, not swallowing, bitter herbs. In church one night, when she was too weak to approach the altar, the Communion bread came to her. Witnesses saw the bread move through the air unassisted. Catherine saw it carried by the hand of Christ.

She died at thirty-three, the same age as her bridegroom at His death. She died in Rome, and her body was venerated from behind an iron grille in a chapel of the Church of the

Minerva, so that the throngs who came would not tear her to bits, each trying to secure a wonder-working relic.

All I have left of my mother are a box of books, a china dog, two cashmere sweaters with holes in the elbows, a few photographs, and her medical records. Among the last of these is her final chest X ray, and just over the shadow of her heart is the bright white circle cast by the saint's medal she wore on a thin gold chain. No matter how many times the technicians asked her to remove it, she would not. Not long ago, I unpacked the box of medical records and retrieved the X ray. I held it before a light once more, trying to see the image more clearly, but of course I could make out nothing. Just a small white circle of brightest light—a circle blocking the view of the chambers of her heart, a circle too bright to allow any vision.

I cannot now remember which saint's image she wore, but I have decided that the medal, now with my mother in her coffin, bears a likeness of Saint Jude. I have given my mother to this saint—the patron of lost causes, the patron of last resort—just as, long ago, she gave me to the saint of her choosing.

INTERIOR CASTLES
II

To encourage immunity to my American environment, I was sent to a prep school whose motto was "College Begins at Two." At that age I was taught to offer my right hand to the school's headmistress while plucking at the side pleat of my gray jumper with my left and bending my knees. In other words, at two I learned to curtsy like a proper British child. By the time I graduated from high school, I'd worn successive sizes of the same navy wool uniform blazer and white oxford shoes for fifteen years, I'd taken six years of Latin, eaten countless Bird's custards and Peek Freans and scones spread with Tiptree Seville Orange marmalade. I'd hidden a decade's worth of smoked tongue sandwiches from my classmates (leaving them in the bottom of my brown lunch bag and throwing them away, still wrapped) and made my way through thousands of Sunday dinners of roast beef, Yorkshire pudding, boiled potatoes, and green beans cooked until they were gray. I spelled color *colour* and said "tomato" the wrong way, and my grandmother could be assured that I was not an "American Brat."

Of course, increasingly, I longed to be exactly that. At school I was as desperate as any other child to fit in, and so being American seemed essential. Brattiness, too, offered seductions to a child raised on didactic British storybooks that featured such cautionary heroines as Rude Polly, stigmatized by large *P*s and *Q*s sewn on all her clothing, one for each Please or Thank You she forgot to say. I saved my weekly allotment of television for Friday night's broadcast of *The Brady Bunch* and *The Partridge Family,* because the children in those shows seemed so American. Based on reports from classmates, *Love, American Style* and *Laugh-In* would have served me even better, but, as my grandmother made clear, those shows were so vulgar that they were broadcast late at night, while decent children were sleeping.

I spent a lot of time alone as a child. The characters in the books I read were very real to me, more than my classmates or neighbors, as were the people in the old photographs in the boxes upstairs: my grandmother and her sister and cousins in Shanghai and in Hong Kong, picnicking on the shores of Japan's Lake Chusengi, or on Lake Como in the Italian Alps. There were others of my quiet grandfather in Germany's Black Forest, fishing in British Columbia (where his brother was a Royal Canadian Mounted Policeman), or in Anchorage, where, in 1915, he worked as a bookkeeper for the Alaska Engineering Commission.

My grandmother's directive that I form myself in opposition to my environment was hardly necessary. Already I understood myself as a creature apart from the other children I met. Not only had I sprung from old-world, other-world, grandparents—my mother's position in relation to me was increasingly sororal, caught as she was in chronic adolescent rebellion—but there was the mystery of my father, whom I never saw and about whom I knew little. If I heard his name, it was in the context of one of the relentless, vicious battles between my mother and my grandmother, arguments that, until I was six and my mother moved out, went on without interruption.

Frightened by the fighting, I took the ready example of my grandmother's home that opposed the world around it and learned to make a similar home within myself, an interior landscape into which I could disappear with increasing ease. This flight was aided, unexpectedly, by my religious instruction. On weekends I was remanded to my mother, who insisted on Saturday ballet lessons and Christian Science Sunday school. An indoctrination that stressed mind over matter with chilling effectiveness, Christian Science was something she'd inherited from my Jewish grandfather, who had been married before, to a Christian Scientist with whom he fell in love when he was twenty-five and living in Anchorage. She died and, perhaps as a form of clandestine mourning, he kept her faith; he passed it on to the child of his second wife, my mother.

This is me, this is you. This is me, this is you. I would whisper this to myself as I sat at the kitchen table, eating breakfast. Or perhaps I only thought the words: a first prayer, a determination to draw a line between myself and the two women I loved. Christian Science doctrine ennobled my desire to ignore anything in my environment that troubled me; it raised denial, that most primitive of human defenses, to a form of worship.

If it became dangerous later on, living inside my head served me well as a young child. I was happy when immersed in fantasy, in storybooks and, later, textbooks. And I loved school, where I was encouraged to be self-contained and where I grew increasingly agile at expressing myself in words, especially those written on paper. It was in school that

I began to create another home—abstract and lacking in material dimension, but utterly manipulable by me—on the page.

When I was eleven we moved from our shabby big house to a smaller one in a less expensive neighborhood. The move was postponed until my grandparents could no longer pay their property taxes, let alone keep the place in repair. My grandfather, whose genius for numbers, for fast and accurate calculation, was paired with profound naïveté, had invested their savings unwisely, buying faltering stocks and turning down a chance to make millions. Given the opportunity, in the forties, to buy a corner lot on the Las Vegas Strip, he decided against it, considering the place too crass and tawdry to ever catch on. And my extravagant mother, who could always solicit a loan as a surrogate for love, had been wasting money with a vengeance.

The new house was, I thought, ugly. It lacked the imaginative details of the one we left, the house my grandparents helped to design and that included hidden cupboards and leaded glass windows made from the round green and brown and blue bottoms of old bottles. The light from these windows poured color into halls and the old foyer, which had a floor of highly polished flagstone, a red and purple Bokhara rug just inside the big front door. This rug was laid on the stones without a pad between, and many times each year someone came in the door and immediately slipped and fell on the shining floor. I'd heard the plumber's skull hit with a thud separate from the impact of his metal toolbox; I'd watched Aunt Pat's purse pop open and spray forth a glittering shower of pillboxes, loose change, lipsticks, smelling salts, gold comb, and a matching compact. Once it was the pediatrician, Dr. Aldrich, fat and sly and sadistic—he'd hide a syringe behind his back and ask if I'd like a "surprise"—but, regretfully, I missed his fall, confined to bed with yet another case of tonsillitis. The three of us, my mother and grandfather and I, were supposed to be Christian Scientists, but my grandmother didn't believe in Mind Over Matter. In fact, she found matter ascendant. When I had a fever she called the doctor.

Matter over mind: the rug looked beautiful on the polished stone floor and there it stayed. "But why didn't she put something underneath, to keep it from slipping?" a friend asked, years later. I shrugged. It was a reasonable question, but one applied to an unreasonable house. She never did. She was kind to the victims, offered ice wrapped in a towel, ginger ale, cups of tea, pieces of shortbread, but the rug, like an outsized banana peel, remained where it was.

In its whimsy, the first house encouraged escapism; the second was just another landscape. To pay off debts, my grandmother sold most of her antiques and carpets—including the murderous one in the foyer—and replaced them with more practical and serviceable things. Long spoiled by eccentricity, both in family and furnishings, I found the attempt at convention confusing. For a year after we moved, I woke up in the morning and didn't recognize my new room with its pale blue rug and one too few windows. The worst of it was the wallpaper chosen by my mother, with climbing vines of huge roses made sinister by the botanical exactitude of their stems and leaves, their saber-like thorns. Realistic or not, the thorns offered the paper no protection; within a few years it was hanging in shreds around the two "cat trees" in my room, feline gymnasiums from whose highest perches kittens rappelled down what was left of the drapes, using their claws to catch threads and swing to the floor.

Even when the cat population dipped to eight or nine, there were always two warring factions. An older generation had full run of the house, with the exception of those rooms in which the younger animals were corralled: my bedroom during the day, and the den during the night. These two rooms were separated by a staircase, up and down which the cats were herded with the incentive of a meal awaiting them at their destination. Transfers were dramatic, if not exactly eventful. Real skirmishes between the older and younger packs were rare, but my histrionic grandmother screamed a lot anyway. "Oh Schatzie! Oh Jessica! Oh Tomita! Come here! Oh! Oh! She's got her by the neck!" In my role as grudging shepherdess, I sometimes drove one herd into another, hoping for diversion, but no more than hisses were exchanged. The cat wars were largely imagined by my combative grandmother. Perhaps, in my mother's absence, the house was too quiet for her.

Of course, my grandmother and I had our own fights, especially about what she considered my abnormal social life, her fears that I was a lesbian. Like her sister, Cecily, whose homosexual love affairs had stigmatized her family, I was bookish and seemingly disinterested in boys, two sure predictors of lesbianism as far as my grandmother was concerned. And I never invited my friends over to our house—not because, as she suspected, we were hiding shameful intimacies, but because there was too much to explain at my house. Too much that was impossible to explain. Tandem litter boxes—three pairs—were one thing, embarrassing but hardly noteworthy in comparison to the bits of raw meat stuck to the door frames, the chairs, and any intact wallpaper. For her cats my grandmother ordered pounds of beef heart and lambs' kidneys from the butcher and picked it up fresh every other day, and she cut the meat by hand into little pieces. Raw organ meat has an adhesive quality, and she got the stuff on her hands and her sleeves, so that she unknowingly anointed whatever she subsequently touched with flecks of raw meat that dried and stuck with surprising tenacity. If I tried to peel one off the wall, the paper came with it.

No one ever won a fight with my grandmother, and as I was as stubborn as she, our inevitable conflicts ended in a draw, always the same, no matter how the argument began. She'd scream, "I took you in! I took you in! You ungrateful girl! Don't you understand, I took you in!" And I'd yell back, "Why don't you throw me out then! Just throw me out! I wish you would!"

Sometimes we were less articulate. My grandmother was superstitious and considered opening an umbrella in the house far more unlucky than breaking a mirror or walking under a ladder. Once, in the throes of a wild rage, I seized my grandfather's big black umbrella from the hall closet, pointed its tip at her heart, and opened it. She screamed and staggered so dramatically that I did it again. And again. Summoned from the garden by the noise inside the house, my grandfather found us, each clinging to one end of the half-furled umbrella. Laughing and crying at once, I had the handle, while she, supporting herself with a chair back, held the point, directing it, like a loaded pistol, away from her body. "I took her in!" she gasped.

"Throw me out!"

We said these things, but (or because) there was no place else I could live. The first time my mother had an apartment that included a room for me was the year I went away to college. I used the room's closet to store clothes I no longer wore, a gesture we both understood as polite. My mother, who never remarried, had for years been locked in a relationship with an alcoholic who never divorced his wife, with whom he had a son my age, a male mirror to my fury and alienation. Not that John and I ever saw one another. We never once shared a meal with his father and my mother. I think all of us suspected we were unequal to the charade of family.

To illustrate how difficult a child John was, my mother told me that he had stolen all the silverware from his mother's kitchen and sold it back to her as she needed it, piece by piece. "Can't we ever get together?" I asked, not the response my mother had imagined—and we didn't—but for years I fantasized about such a meeting, the chance to congratulate John or, better still, apprentice myself to the mastermind of so elegant a campaign of manipulation.

I understand now, as I did not in the days that I was treading carefully over her carpets that bore fresh vacuum tracks, that superficial order was what my mother needed to shroud the waste of her youth and beauty and intelligence. At the time, she made me feel like Pig Pen from the *Peanuts* comic strip, someone around whom swirled clouds of dust and grime. When I looked into her mercilessly polished mirrors, I never saw a face but a composite of mascara smudges, stray hairs, and misplaced freckles. I slept at my mother's only a few times, and on each of those nights home from college, after she'd gone to bed I'd lock myself in the bathroom, sit on the counter with my feet in the sink, and squeeze clogged pores on my nose and chin until they bled, something I couldn't do in a cramped dorm room or the vast and drafty communal bathrooms.

I took three years off between college and graduate school. During those years, both my mother and my grandfather were dying. It was time given to memorizing rather than to grief, which makes its own appointments. I was trying to learn all I could of what—who—would be taken from me. I wanted to be left with at least an accounting of what was lost. But the deathwatch required a sort of self-imposed anesthesia. What I felt penetrated only so far; I didn't allow it to touch me, hidden as I was, deep inside myself.

One day I came home from the hospital to have tea with my grandmother, but when I entered the kitchen, my grandmother didn't have the kettle on the stove, there were no cups or cookies on the table. She held a sheaf of papers in her lap. "Why didn't you ever show me these!" she said.

I shrugged. "What are they?"

"I found them in your desk. Years worth! And you never showed me one. Why?"

I took what she handed to me: twenty-four gold honor roll certificates, one earned each quarter of every school year from the seventh grade through the twelfth. "I don't know," I said.

But I remembered bringing them home from school and, without showing them to anyone, hiding them in the drawer of the desk where I'd earned them. When the stack got too high, I threw out the thick envelopes in which each had been presented. My life at school, an interior life, writing papers and earning the grades that ultimately made me valedictorian, was private. I did my homework alone, behind closed doors, and when my grandfather offered me rewards for straight A's, I turned them down. They were mine, those A's, and couldn't be bought. Report cards, certificates, letters of acceptance to colleges and universities—had my grandmother looked, she would have found these in another drawer—were documents of a life I guarded against my family.

"I'm surprised you went through my desk," I said, and my grandmother put her face in her hands and cried.

In graduate school I met the man I would marry, though when I arrived in Iowa City I was preoccupied with the past, hardly acknowledging a future, which, in any case, I was too tired to consider. I went to the university housing office to pick up a list of possible rooms to rent. The first, owned by Mrs. K., a widow, was listed at $140 a month, furnished. It was on the top floor of her small clapboard house on Ronald Street, and its ceiling sloped steeply over the twin bed on one side and the chest of drawers on the other, so steeply that you couldn't prop a mirror on the dresser, nor could you sit up in bed to read. The bed's frame was iron and evoked sanitoria dormitories; its mattress was very soft. Getting out would mean rolling out, toward the center of the room, where the ceiling was higher. The room's molding, baseboard, and doors were all painted mustard yellow, a choice inspired, I concluded, by the wallpaper, whose design of black and green and brown and yellow paisley was so hideous that it made my big shredded roses, still hanging in my grand-mother's house, look almost pretty. The walls and ceiling of the room were covered in bilious swirls printed unevenly on the paper, their black outlines missing their colored middles by as much as a quarter of an inch. To look more than pass-ingly at this two-dimensional rendering of nausea, or of des-perate depression, induced eyestrain and then vertigo.

The toilet and shower were on the first floor, which Mrs. K. shared with the downstairs boarder, a slight Korean woman studying engineering—I never learned her name. And there was, Mrs. K. showed me, an auxiliary toilet in the spider-infested basement. Set in the middle of the cracked and sweating concrete floor, among cobwebbed boxes and broken, mildewed chairs, it had a plastic shower curtain that could be drawn around it for privacy.

The pinched bedroom, its awful wallpaper, the visit to

the dank basement: none of these galvanized me, as they would today, into a search for a less dispiriting home. Instead, Mrs. K.'s basement seemed to leach the last reserves of my energy; climbing back into the light, I realized I didn't have whatever it might take to save myself from another home so peculiar and embarrassing that I wouldn't consider asking friends over.

I signed a year's lease, agreeing to take the room and thus to share a tiny kitchen and eating area with A., the other upstairs boarder. A. had the nicer bedroom, painted blue with a large window alcove and hanging plants. The week I moved in, A. was visiting her family, so all I could glean of her was that suggested by the few personal effects in the blue bedroom. The bookshelf by the bed, neatly made, tucked tight, held a King James translation of the Bible, eleven self-help books, one Adele Davis cookbook, a variety of analgesics, and a box of pink scented Kleenex. On the back of her door hung pajamas and a plaid bathrobe. When A. herself arrived, she told me she had been an undergraduate for seven years, so far, without declaring a major. I soon learned that the work that A. found more engrossing than her studies was the maintenance of a detailed health log, a daily, sometimes hourly journal of her premenstrual symptoms, and a condition newly identified by American doctors: TMJ, or temporal-mandibular-joint syndrome, which A. believed was contributing to her incapacitating headaches.

A. didn't share the journal's entries with me, but she left it open on the table at which we ate our separate meals. And, as this seemed to me a tacit invitation, I read the entries, as many as I could stand. Then I went into my room and lay on Mrs. K.'s iron bed and looked at the paisley wallpaper and observed that, for the first time in my life, I lived in an environment that reflected how I felt, at least in those months following my mother's death, when I was as flat and dizzy, as unfocusedly black and brown and green and yellow as the terrible walls around me. I went to classes, did the work required of me, socialized halfheartedly with other students, walked up and down and around the few streets of the college town, often not seeing houses or people or even the twisting river because my mind filled abruptly with an intimate and frightening clutter of bedpans, catheters, sores that would not heal, oxygen tubes and pills of all colors, enough medication to require a written dosage schedule; it was too complicated to rely on memory. All of these scrolled through my head silently, like slides.

At Mrs. K.'s house, I closed my bedroom door behind me, coming out only at night, while A. and Mrs. K. and the Korean girl slept. I made tea on the burner and drank it at the little table placed between refrigerator and sink. If there had been an oven, I would have done what my grandmother forbade, set it to broil and rested my feet on its open door. I examined the food A. kept on her shelf of the refrigerator. Sometimes I tasted what she brought home from her parents' house, slices of turkey and cold potatoes left over from family dinners. I'd peel away an inconspicuous shred of flesh and chew it slowly. Rather than go downstairs or into the horrible basement, I peed in the sink—an acrobatic transgression, I had to climb onto the counter and over the dish drainer—and by that feral gesture I made the kitchen mine.

I felt a mean delight in doing something I knew would horrify A., whom I had begun to hate for losing herself in obsessive worries about her body. Would I have had more compassion for her suffering were I not myself enduring the tenth year of chronically relapsing anorexia, my own secret notebooks given over to calories consumed, exercise accomplished. "Ten years," I'd whisper to my reflection in the mirror. "Ten," trying to frighten the woman I saw, the one who had spent a decade within the careful confines of self-denial, a decade within a deliberate internal architecture assembled to protect and contain. I hated A. because she provided a vision of myself more valid, and damning, than what I saw in Mrs. K.'s mirror, its silver backing peeling off in circles and offering a fragmented image, unreliable as that cast back by a pond's ruffled surface.

Can you see yourself in a mirror the way you can in someone's eyes? When, on our third date, my future husband came up Mrs. K.'s stairs, Colin's expression of surprise and, worse, pity made me abruptly aware of the room in which I lived. He spent one night on the awful bed, and the next morning he handed me his house key. We never discussed our living together before I moved in, any more than we talked about marriage or parenthood before they were done. Certainly we loved one another, but we'd loved other people. Our bond was that we recognized each other, completed one another. I knew with whom, if not how, to make a home, and took it as a betrothal when we shelved our books together and discarded the duplicates.

We moved from Iowa to New York with a small U-Haul truck filled with boxes of books, a bed, two desks, and five thrift-store chairs—all of which were together worth less money than it cost to transport them. Their value was that they were ours, they were what we shared. Colin drove the truck; I flew ahead of him to find an apartment in New York City. I had five days. The place I chose was in Brooklyn and included a tiny garden in which Colin grew tomatoes and basil, cucumbers, zucchini, and even a few token ears of Iowa corn. The garden was crowded, but inside, the few rooms were only half filled by our things. A friend donated a couch; we bought a table and bookshelves at IKEA: bland things of unpainted wood. The apartment never transcended its haphazard, junky quality, and we lived in it for only two years.

As we sat together at Colin's parents' dining table, addressing envelopes for wedding invitations, Colin's mother suggested that I register for gifts. There were so many things we needed, and others that we didn't. I agreed, very tepidly, and put off the chore because (I thought) I was uncomfortable suggesting to friends and family what they might buy for us. But wasn't the deeper discomfort that I had little sense, really, of what made a household? When a friend, the same who gave us her couch, realized that I might never accomplish the trip alone, she forcibly accompanied me to Bloomingdale's, where vistas of beds and sofas invited stupor. I walked behind Lori, resisting the urge to take her hand. How easy to sink into cushions, fall as deeply asleep as Dorothy in the narcotic embrace of the poppy field separating her from Oz's Emerald City, and from what she longs for: to find her way home.

Beyond beds were housewares, table after table set with empty plates and glasses and looking to me like a judgment: a sneering jibe at someone who so many times had refused food, especially in company. If what I ended up selecting proved useful, it was only that I responded, zombielike, to sensible promptings.

Once we were married, Colin and I moved into a brownstone that my grandmother helped us to buy and that included a ground-floor apartment in which she lived for the last two years of her life. Her furniture, shipped east from Los Angeles, overflowed its rooms into those above, and it wasn't until we built a house on the north fork of Long Island that, for the first time in my life, I had to face the task of filling an empty house. It was a second home, a place to be used only during the summer and for weekends, but still, we needed furniture on which to sleep, sit, eat. We needed shower curtains, wastebaskets, wineglasses. We needed a refrigerator and a stove. Though I was in my thirties, the mother of two children, though the summer house was to be the fifth home I shared with my husband, I'd never before had to consider all that went into a home. What was required, and what was comfort. I showed little aptitude for the task. I bought appliances and beds, a secondhand dining table, chairs, and couch, and then inertia set in. Or was it paralysis?

Five years later, I'd made little progress. In apology for the missing chests of drawers, I gave everyone a twelve-pack of plastic hangers from the supermarket. What clothes we couldn't hang or throw over closet rods, we dropped on the floor. I left my underwear and nightgown in my overnight bag, as if to announce what I felt: that I'd only just arrived. The children, who, as it turned out, were not yet tall enough to reach the hangers, each had a box to hold underwear, pajamas, clothes.

I could have bought dressers at IKEA, where Colin and I went to buy beds, but I didn't want all the furniture to match; I thought it would look like we lived in a motel. At least that's what I told Colin afterward, but at IKEA I was speechless. I fought the dangerous desire to lie down in the guise of testing the firmness of a mattress and tried to complete one of the little white forms we were given at the entrance to the immense warehouse. It looked like a scorecard for miniature golf, and came with a stubby, eraserless pencil but was intended to be filled with the stock numbers of the items we wanted. Colin asked me questions, simple ones like: "How about this?" which I met in glazed silence. At some point he took off alone, in frustration, and I sat in a chair the color of oatmeal and watched the children, who used bunk beds as gym equipment, until he returned and I gave him my scorecard, unchanged from when he last looked it over.

The one room of the summer house that I outfitted fully was the one in which I wrote. It had a table and a chair, a shelf for books. A neighbor, after visiting several times and noting that the walls remained unadorned, invited me to select what I wanted of her paintings, stored in her basement. Sensing my inertia, she escorted me home with three and watched as I drove nails into the plaster.

"How about here?" she said, trying to guide my hammer to the blank white wall of the study that my chair faced. But I resisted. I didn't dislike her painting, an abstract of red and blue, but I hung it on the wall I never see, the one at my back.

I still live in my work. I make the page my home, just as I did when a schoolgirl, writing book reports, history essays. I carry drafts of novels out to dinner, the movies, even the market. When I travel, I open my folders on planes and trains and in unfamiliar rooms in countries whose languages and food are unknown, and I feel at home, immediately comfortable.

There are dangers to interior castles, I know. I find my thoughts return to the one frank conversation I had with my mother in the last year of her life. In trying to explain why she had always been so remote, my mother told me that inside herself she had discovered a fortress, assembled brick by psychic brick to defend herself against my grandmother. "The problem is," she said, starting to cry, "I don't know the way out. I'm stuck inside myself."

What were they made of, my mother's internal walls? An obsession with order and cleanliness, with polished surfaces and tasteful things placed just so. An opera aria—Puccini not Wagner—a shimmering edifice of perfectly rendered female notes: emotion she could enjoy without owning, enjoy because it was not hers. A hollandaise even better than the last and the right wine to complement it. My mother's was a system, like my own anorexia, that delivered safety in perfection, and that purposefully left no openings.

And what of a writer's walls of language? Must I remain vigilant to ensure that what I've built inside myself continues to be a home and not a trap? Is it safe to assume that if words can make a wall, they can also make a door, the passage out, or, for readers, in?

KEEPING TIME

One on the bookshelf behind the bed. One on the desk, between the pencil mug and the printer. Another in the kitchen, between canisters of rice and flour. A fourth in the bathroom, next to the Q-Tips. A fifth on the mantel. A sixth by the phone. One in my satchel; another in the pocket of my winter coat. Two in a closet, awaiting new batteries. It used to be that I had even more.

Lorus. Braun. Linden. Swiss Army. The brand is irrelevant, the features interchangeable: Black plastic case, with a hinged cover that flips back to double as a stand. Black analogue dial, no more than two inches in diameter. Arabic numerals highlighted in wan, phosphorescent green. Hands powered by a single AA battery.

I've been advised of a few cardinal rules for insomniacs: If you wake, don't check the time. If you can't fall back to sleep, get up, read, listen to music, take a bath. Whatever you do, never lie in bed watching the inexorable progress of the hours as they traverse the face of a bedside alarm. But never mind waking, I can't fall asleep without a clock at arm's length. Nor, apparently, can I write, cook, shower, talk on the phone, go to the library, or sit in my living room apart from the silent blind gaze of one of these inscrutable little faces.

And who's watching whom? After all, preoccupied as I am with time, its flights and ebbs and cruel grinds, I can almost always guess not just the hour but the minute hand's position. Without a wristwatch I am just as punctual—i.e., early—as with. Minutes misspent fill me with anxiety, even despair, and though I can't claim to never waste time, I always know how much.

In my early forties, and in good health, I admit to an exaggerated sense of mortality. My mother died young. Her parents, who raised me, are dead now as well. I grew up witness to the failing of flesh; as a child in my grandparents' house, I didn't have the comfort of believing I'd live forever. In that house, too, were many clocks—one on each mantel, a grandfather in the hall—but these were big clocks that ticked loudly through the dark hours. Listening to them from my bed, the hourly chorus of chimes and strikes and the one forlorn and wheezing cuckoo's call, I would feel the breath pressed from my lungs. Like the clocks, like the grandparents, I, too, would eventually wind down.

Still, my clock watching is not so simple as the apprehension of death. My mother was one of those women who lived her short, pretty life outside of the constraints of time—in flagrant disobedience to time—at least as it was marked by the wristwatch, the mantel clock, the grandfather listing toward the stairs. It wasn't that she was late in any prosaic sense. No, in tardiness, as in other areas, she was grand, extravagant, epic. Late by an hour, a day, a season.

Late for church, late for work, even late for love. My mother left dates honking in their cars, pacing in the hall, or sitting on my grandparents' sofa, big men folded up like paper dolls, knees higher than their heads as their buttocks sagged through broken springs, down as far as their heels. I'd sit in the foyer, on the staircase's bottom tread, the perfect vantage from which to observe her arrival into the living room.

Alerted by the herald of high heels striking the hall floor, my mother's date would be working to free himself from the dusty chintz cushions, hauling himself up by the creaking sofa arm, grabbing for the edge of the coffee table, or, as one memorably did, rolling forward and sideways onto the carpet. He dusted himself off before offering her his arm.

But none of it was funny when I was the one who was waiting. Always the last to be picked up from birthday parties, Sunday school, ballet class, dental appointments, each year I had a hundred opportunities to practice nonchalance.

"Don't worry. I'm sure she's on her way," other mothers promised. Teachers offered paper, colored pencils; receptionists brought me paper cups of water. I'd thank these women without meeting their eyes, knowing as I did how a stranger's compassion could be a catalyst for tears. And I couldn't cry, because when I did, it embarrassed my mother; it made her angry. As soon as the two of us were safe inside the car, windows rolled tight, she'd yell while I held my breath, my eyes not on her face but on that of the dashboard clock, always stopped or wrong. Midnight. Yesterday. Next year.

My mother's turquoise Pontiac announced itself as the vehicle of a fugitive, backseat filled with clothes shrouded in dry-cleaning bags, an overnight case and makeup kit, a hair dryer with its domed bonnet latched tight. The tape deck played eight-tracks; over and over José Feliciano keened *Come on baby light my fire.* Sometimes he got through the final verse before she took a bump too fast; then the mechanism would eject the black plastic cartridge into the backseat with dangerous force, sufficient to black an eye. Long before she moved out, my mother's car and its broken clock told me to study how it felt when she was late. One day, it warned, she wouldn't show up at all; the bedroom next to mine would be unoccupied.

By her bed, the ice blue glow of her Westclox alarm spilled onto an uncreased white pillowcase. After she left home, I'd come into her room at night to put my ear close to the clock's warm case, close enough to listen to what its contemptuous electric buzz might tell me. Was there any loss that an adjustment of time—an hour more, a minute less— couldn't cure? The sly gold needle of its circling second hand stitched the minutes into place, one and then another.

I got my first travel alarm when I was in college. I found it in an airport store, the kind that sells sewing kits and tampons and Alka-Seltzer, overpriced remedies for mishaps of travel. I wasn't going anywhere, just wandering through the terminal while waiting to meet my mother's flight, which was, of course, late—I imagined whole airlines, the lives of hundreds of strangers, disrupted by her cosmic conflict with schedules. The salesgirl removed the clock from the display case and handed it to me. I watched one revolution of its second hand—one minute I had held—and then bought it. I liked the way the clock, so compact, slipped into my pocket, liked touching its square case through the fabric of my denim jacket. Back at school I kept it in my satchel, rarely taking it out to check the time (after all, I wore a watch) but still enamored of its size and its silence. What I liked most was carrying a little clock among my books and papers, bearing away the hours even as they bore me away.

Soon I had two; then, suddenly, ten, twenty. They were cheap, as addictions go, and typically I fell prey to them during times of strain, times when others might have wanted a drink, but me, I wanted the time. Now their number is declining. Some were lost, a few broke, and after I had children I stopped buying new ones. You see, even before the first dance recital, I discovered that it is children, like the child I once was, who are the most faithful, and relentless, timekeepers.

TICK

"So, do people get run over by cars and then God, who is invisible, just picks them up from where they are all flat and bloody and he throws them into heaven?" my daughter asks. "Is that what happens?" She holds out her hands, palms upturned in a gesture of inquiry and impatience.

Sarah's theories of the afterlife are marked by athleticism—sudden changes of spiritual status accomplished by God's bouncing or kicking souls from one world to another. She's a defender of reincarnation, thinks of heaven as a waiting room, and claims that women are impregnated when God hurls souls of the recently dead into empty female stomachs.

"Is that what you think happens?" I ask. Sarah shrugs, drops her hands to her sides.

"I'm asking you," she says. "I know what I think."

I go on brushing my daughter's hair. We're standing before the window, looking out on a field bright with wildflowers. Arranged on the windowsill are the hair ornaments that Sarah has selected for the day: a set of pink barrettes, three green elastic ponytail holders, a fake tortoiseshell headband, and two ribbons. In sum, many too many decorations for one small head.

I brush longer than I need to. The tangles are out and the brushing soothes me with its repetitive motion, like sewing or sweeping or fucking, late-night, too-tired-to-fuck fucking.

"Hold still," I say to my daughter.

"I hate this," Sarah says.

"I know," I say. "Everyone does."

I gather the mass of my daughter's hair, pull it back over her shoulders. "Hold still," I say again. It's quixotic to embark on a French braid without having a television to tranquilize my five-year-old daughter, but that's also what makes these braids so beautiful on a small, always moving head: the very impossibility of them. I pick up the first handful of hair and weave in sections from the side, moving down the back of her skull. An undetected snarl halts my progress, and I reach for the hairbrush, which falls from the windowsill. I hold the hair with one hand while I stoop to retrieve the brush.

"Did Daddy make a hole in you with his penis?" Sarah asks.

"No!" I say. "What do you mean?"

"Well, at school they said that babies come from seeds planted in the mother, and that the mother has a egg and that the fathers plant the seeds and that they do it with their penises, so what I mean is, is the penis like the little shovel thing that you use to make a hole before you plant a seed. That's what I mean."

"Oh," I say. "The fathers don't have to make a hole because the mothers have a place for the seed to go in. Everything is all ready for the seed."

"Is it your mouth? Do you swallow it and then it grows in your stomach?"

"No," I say. "It's the place between your legs. The seed goes in the same place that the baby comes out. We talked about this before."

We've talked about it a lot, because this summer all we talk about is sex and death, something I'll regard with unexpected nostalgia when we reach the next of humankind's compelling topics: excrement.

As I braid, my fingers encounter something soft and slightly flabby just behind Sarah's right ear. A kernel of corn, I think. Every night in the country we've eaten corn, and the children attack it messily, shearing the bright-yellow buttons off the cob with their sharp little teeth so that half of them drop into their laps and onto the floor. I hold the unfinished braid in my left hand and search through Sarah's hair with my right. I've found corn kernels in the couch and in the beds—even in their shoes. The thing on Sarah's scalp is the size of a large kernel and has a stale, liverish yellow color, but it doesn't brush away. I bend over to look more closely. It's a tick, so engorged that its color has gone from brown to yellow: it has swallowed so much blood that it is pale with intemperance.

I drop the hair I'm holding. Involuntarily, my hand rushes to cover my mouth in a cinematic gesture of shock and revulsion, one I find absurd even in its helplessness. Sarah is engrossed in watching the woodchuck that lives by the compost heap—he's dragging off one of last night's corn-cobs—so I have a moment to collect myself in the bathroom before I have to gather what I need: tweezers, hydrogen peroxide, cotton balls.

Sarah's hair hangs to her waist and naturally attracts trouble: burrs and gum and pine tar and glue. There's not much that hasn't got stuck in it before. So why am I on my knees on the bath mat, tears dripping into my lap? "Don't be silly!" I would say if it had been Sarah who began to cry. "You're a big girl."

In the cluttered bathroom, toys and toiletries strewn over the floor, my son, three years old, looks up from his clandestine occupations. I can see only one of Walker's eyes behind the big Superman mask he's wearing, its eyeholes cut too far apart to accommodate both of his eyes simultaneously. Seeing that I'm too preoccupied to scold or impede him, he returns with satisfaction to unfolding the towels, all of which he dumps into the damp bathtub. By the window, Sarah is standing still. Her hair has fallen back over the tick, hiding it, and her face is rapt and beautiful, bathed in clear morning light. I move behind her and, with the tweezers, part her hair to expose the tick.

"Mom!" she wails. I have the tweezers clenched on what looks like the head of the tick and I'm pulling hard, bracing myself with my left hand planted securely against the crown of my daughter's head. But the tick is not letting go; its hold is preternaturally fierce. Just inside the grip of the metal pincers, the bloated bag of the tick's body seeps blood. Sarah's A-positive life wells up around the eight flailing legs of the tick. I pull harder, and the legs stop moving. They stiffen, as if with resolve. I twist it a little, hoping to loosen the animal's jaws or fangs or mandibles—whatever mechanism it has for holding on so tightly. My hand is slick with sweat, the tweezers begin to slip in my fingers.

"Mom! Mom! Mom!" my daughter cries. What could have possessed her mother, she must wonder, to turn a morning braid into this torment?

"I'm sorry, sweetie," I say, my voice unnaturally chipper. "There's something stuck in your hair. I just have to get it out."

Don't pull the body off the head! Don't pull the body off the head! I tell myself. Sarah struggles against my left hand, which still holds her skull tightly, and against my thighs and pelvis, which pin her to the windowsill so she cannot escape. If she gets away, she'll go under the bed or hide in the deep, out-of-reach corner of the linen closet, the way she does when she gets a scrape and I go after her with the disinfectant. She isn't weirdly, improbably stoic like her little brother, now standing silent in the doorway between bathroom and bedroom, staring at the two of us. Sarah regards most parental interventions as acts of unwarranted aggression.

The tick comes free, and she collapses sobbing on the bed. "I hate you!" she screams, choking on tears.

In the bathroom I dump the toothbrushes from their mug and drop the tick inside. I debate whether to show my daughter the animal and vindicate my behavior or to protect her from the knowledge of the vileness of ticks. Sarah is in one of her frightened periods. She is afraid of things she knows—fire, dogs, spiders, worms, candle smoke, and vaccinations—and of things of which she has heard but of whose horror she cannot quite conceive: earthquakes, vampire bats, and appendicitis. Wherever we go—her grandparents', the beach, the supermarket, or, as we did one week at the end of winter, Florida—she asks, hesitating distrustfully before disembarking from car or train or bus or plane, "Are there earthquakes here?"

Already Sarah suspects that grown-ups lie to protect her from her fears—when they aren't lying to trick her into obedience—and she considers their answers to her questions darkly, her small eyebrows meeting in fierce appraisal. I decide to show her the tick, but when she looks into the mug she's unimpressed and scowls at me. I have to sit on my daughter to clean the tick bite with peroxide, which foams around the small bloody place on her scalp. Her heel goes into my crotch with angry force. She calls me a witch and says that I am ugly and *spiteful,* a word I threw at her just last night. Sarah will spend the rest of the morning putting on puppet shows for her little brother. In each production, the witch puppet will be killed by Red Riding Hood: once by fire, twice by drowning, and many times by being plunged to her death from a cliff provided by a staircase behind the theater.

In another part of the house, I pursue my own drama. The tick lies on its back on the bottom of the blue toothbrush mug. If I discount the mouth and legs, its body's shape and color really are exactly those of a large, stale kernel of corn, a resemblance I find repellent.

Fat with greed, the tick moves its legs with languid strokes of gluttony, as if it were swimming slowly in my child's warm blood. I thought that in removing it I had dealt the tick a mortal wound, because when I squeezed and pulled, a red bead of blood—Sarah's—formed bright on its dull underside. But the blood it lost seems now to have been reabsorbed, sucked back in through the little pore that surrendered it.

Under the tick's back, cloudy stains of toothpaste render its imprisonment in the blue china mug absurdly celestial. And this, along with the delighted, drunken motions of the animal's legs, makes me cruel as well as angry. I flip on the overhead light, a collective three hundred watts that reveal the striations on the tick's body. They look like flattened pleats, places where, accordionlike, its body expanded as its hunger was satisfied. *How will I kill it?* I think.

On the shelf above the toilet are manicure tools in a red leather case, each implement secured under a tiny girdle of red elastic—a long-ago present from my mother. I select a shiny, stainless steel wand, a genteel device for nudging back cuticles. When I press the tip of it into the tick the metal descends into the strangely leathery button of the thing. The tick, motionless, doesn't betray any suffering. I push harder, feeling sick to my stomach. *Perhaps I should just drown it in rubbing alcohol,* I think. But I'm committed to the idea of punishment. Vengeance makes little sense against a tiny adversary that may not even register its pain, but it is what I want.

We received a set of steak knives as a wedding gift and never used them. Heavy handled, with blades as narrow as stilettos', the knives are dangerously unbalanced. *I will poke the tip of one of them into the tick,* I think, moving tentatively toward the kitchen, the mug held gingerly out from my side. *I will stick the point of the knife into that place where the blood oozed out before, that sort of tick asshole.* Or I could pull out the legs. Or cut them off with the scalpel-like knife. But, I think, standing in the quiet kitchen, those knives aren't in the drawer, are they? No, they're in one of the cryptically marked cartons in the basement. This is our first summer in the country house, and I have yet to move our things into their proper places.

I shake the mug, and the tick bounces around inside like a bean. It draws its legs in tightly against its liverish sides. A tick is not an insect, I recall from high school invertebrate biology. A tick has eight legs and is related to spiders and crabs. A tick wants blood more than anything, I know, and as I say the words to myself, as I articulate the tick's longing, I understand what I myself want: to make it bleed, to make it surrender what it stole from my child. It's not that I demand this creature's imagined remorse, but what was Sarah's must be returned. A nervous, cool dread uncoils within me.

There's no point in tearing through all those boxes for the steak knives, so I select another kitchen tool, a mysterious implement that resembles an attenuated nutpick. Whatever it is and wherever it came from, I've never had need of it before and won't mind discarding it after this one profane use.

I cut off the first segment of the tick's right foreleg, my determined barbarism making my scalp tighten. I put the pick down, my hand straying unconsciously to the place above my right ear, touching the spot on my own head where the tick bit Sarah. When I pick up the implement again, I'm not aware of my hand shaking, but the tip of the pick wavers so that it's hard to pin down the rest of the leg and separate it from the body. The tick draws its other limbs into its sides, curls them so tightly that they look like the dots on a ladybug. Lying beside its own amputated joints, it betrays no pain or dismay, just the resolve that other legs will not be so mistreated.

When the phone rings, I almost drop the mug. *"What?"* I say.

"Kathryn?" says my husband, at work in the city.

"Yes," I say. "Hi."

"What's up?"

"Nothing. I found a tick on Sarah."

"Oh," he says, sounding unconcerned. "A big one or a little one?"

"Big."

"Well, that's good, right? It's the little ones that are bad."

"The Lyme ones are little," I concede. "But they're all bad."

Colin tells a tick-related anecdote about his boyhood dog. Understanding that this is intended to relieve my anxiety, I pretend that it does. I tilt the mug back and forth, rolling my wrist so that the tick makes slow circles around the perimeter of the bottom. What is happening inside that tiny, secret brain? Dizziness? Fear? Pain? At least one of these, I hope. I stop swirling the tick in the mug and check to see if it's still moving. It is.

I remember suddenly where I'll find the steak knives. They didn't fit into the last kitchen-miscellany box, so I put them with the books. I slipped the flat box of knives between Garrison Keillor and Milan Kundera, a slot where they seemed, during a punch-drunk phase of packing, to make an apt transition—Keillor, Knives, Kundera—dividing the two kinds of humor. In the box is also the unreadably compact, two-volume edition of the *Oxford English Dictionary,* still in its dark blue case, which includes a drawer with a magnifying glass.

"So," Colin says. "How's it going? You working on your book?"

"Fine," I say. "Yes," I lie. We talk for a few more minutes, and then I go down to the basement, leaving the cordless phone on the stairs, where I won't remember to find it the next time it rings. I tear open the tape on the carton. The steak knives are there, just where I pictured them. I slide out the little drawer of the OED's case and take the magnifying glass as well.

The tick is using its last leg to cling to the blade of a steak knife, a surface that the magnifying glass reveals to be utterly smooth, lacking any hold for purchase. The tick trembles in the air but magically does not fall. I am pitting myself against a tiny creature of pure instinct, a button programmed for survival, a blot of life unaffected by hope or fear, a fleck of animate energy with an admirable reluctance to die.

We must have rubbing alcohol somewhere, I know we do; but I can't find it, so from the cupboard I get a bottle of white Island rum, a gift from my husband's parents, recently returned from Saint Croix. I twist off the sticky lid and pour the heavy liquid out over the tick, and it has a strangely clarifying effect. The rum brings the tick horribly close to my eye, so close that the bloated gut seems planetary in its hugeness. Yes, huge: there is nothing bigger in the world than this tick stuffed with its minute apparatuses of consumption and digestion.

The surface of the gut consists of gradations of pigment, variances both subtle and extreme. I'm mesmerized by the tick's belly, its topography of shadow and light. The tiny orb becomes, suddenly, a moon. One smudge unmistakably recalls the largest of the lunar landscape's shadows, the Sea of Tranquillity, or whatever it's called—Sea of Longing, of Lonesomeness. All those dim, blue bodies of un-water. When long-dead astronomers peered through their antique, imperfect telescopes, they thought of water: *Mare Undarum,* Sea of Waves. *Mare Serenitatis,* Sea of Fair Weather. But I always get the names wrong. Sea of Loneliness, I think, Sea of Trepidation, of Solemnity. Colin shakes his head. "Why such sad names?" my husband asks.

The rum has dissolved the toothpaste, and the tick floats in a blue the color of a suburban pool. Its one remaining leg curls and uncurls, making a tiny hook, like a beckoning black finger. What passes for its head has gained complexity and even features in the bath of rum. It looks wise and ancient, innocent by virtue of its primitiveness. It looks like the head on a pre-Columbian sculpture squatting under thick museum glass. Like an icon, the tick cares nothing for its incidental, man-made environment. Its kind existed centuries before me and will persist for centuries hence. Ticks evolved to their present state as soon as there was warm-blooded life to support them. And why should they change? In response to what threat? I have taken more than an hour not yet to kill one.

Does it breathe? It survives, missing seven legs and submerged in the alcohol. Why is its desire to live so unbeatable?

I consider whether I ought to push the blade into the tick's belly while it lies on its back, aiming for that tiny anus or whatever that little hole is, or do what seems less grisly and shove the blade through its back. I swirl the rum in the mug, and the tick turns from its back to its belly. Dorsal, ventral. Decent words of erudition. Civilized words from twelfth-grade science class dissections of frogs, rats, worms.

I pin the tick belly down. The blade skids off until I lodge it in one of the creases left from its expandable pleats. Surprisingly, pressure does not rupture what's left of the body; instead, an elegant silver stream of bubbles erupts from each of the seven places where I tore a leg off. I push the knife harder, and it goes in at last with a tiny pop. But still no blood. I withdraw the knife's blade and use the handle to press on the tick until a fat, black bubble—of what? intestine?—exudes through the hole I made in the tick's skin. Its exoskeleton.

I am waiting for Sarah's blood to drift into the rum, to waft pinkly over the tiny corpse. The reappearance of my daughter's stolen life will qualify as redemption. That's why I have performed this abomination. But, though I have made ten holes in the tick with the fine point of the blade, and from each of them pressed a tarry bubble, I have not drawn blood. The tick's leg curls and uncurls, each tiny jointed segment beautiful in its persistent perfection. The body is a mess. Pulped. Nothing left to plunder. All of what the tick drank from my daughter is digested, evidently; Sarah's blood has turned to excrement before I could reclaim it.

In the bathroom, I consider the dismembered submarine carnage of torn legs and what seem like trailing intestines that undulate in the rum. Cloudy now instead of clear, the spirit reveals my cruelty as a dulling process: one of obfuscation. I lift the toilet lid and pour the rum into the water. The pieces of tick sink, sliding slowly down the concave incline of the white bowl.

The tick has won.

SIVA'S DAUGHTERS

"I'll eat you up!" my grandmother would cry. "I'll have you on toast! You'll be the jam!"

She frightened me, this woman who raised me, and not only because she wanted to consume whoever and whatever she loved, but because from the beginning I knew we were the same: everything we felt, we felt furiously.

Our house itself was mad. She loved cats, so we had seventeen. She loved Chanel No. 5, she loved dark red, she loved steak and Lindt bittersweet chocolate—she loved these all so well that she never considered other scents or colors or flavors; it was clear that she would drown herself in these. When she bought another kind of chocolate, it was only to make sure that it was less desirable. The pleasure of her brief infidelity was that it reconfirmed her passion for Lindt bittersweet.

Raised by such a woman, I was not taught to temper my nature; I succumbed to my own furious loves and went out into the world to follow them. But I always came back; I couldn't stay away from my grandmother for long, and I'd pick her up to hug her. She hated that; she'd kick and I liked to feel her kicking.

Passion isn't tender; it's not kind, unless kindness is bait: Passion can appear kind for as long as it takes to ensnare its object. Those of us at the mercy of a passionate nature are children of Siva, a Hindu god with four arms, wrapped in tiger skin, mounted on a bull: god of paradox, savior of those he doesn't annihilate, chief among vampires.

The vampire is our mascot and our caution: lustful monster, creature who loves life too much to bear to part with it, who loves it so foolishly that he ends up damned to eternal unlife, to unslakable thirst. Those afflicted by passion always want to eat or drink up the object of their desire, because what—who—they love (or hate) inspires such intensity of feeling, they are afraid it will obliterate them. It's eat or be eaten.

My grandmother and I made ourselves sick on Lindt bittersweet chocolate, on that and on other loves.

MINOR SURGERIES

The cats my grandmother kept were purebred Himalayans, with the squat bodies, long coats, and squashed faces of Persians, the markings of Siamese. "Colourpoints," they were called in Britain, where the breed was established by Mrs. S. M. Harding—"a real egghead" in my grandmother's opinion: this was a compliment. Night after night she sat on the couch, trying to read Mrs. Harding's books and articles on hybridization, finding them incomprehensible and tedious. In her frustration she was possessed with desire for a cat bred by S. M. Harding. Inside this animal would be a distillate of the woman's genius, something my grandmother regarded more as potent spell than messy snarl of DNA. Having a Harding cat would free her from understanding the complexities of crossbreeding and allow her to effortlessly produce kittens that would win Best of Breed at the Santa Monica Cat Show.

She had two Himalayans already, animals she bought from Marguerita Goforth, the American pioneer of the breed, but they were old now. Spayed and fat and lazy, they did badly in the judge's circle; their noses were too long, their ears too big: "pet quality" in the vernacular of the Southern California Himalayan Society, of which my grandmother was a recent member. The group of fifteen or twenty women met once a month at one of the members' houses, and for this exacting audience my grandmother wanted an enviable "show" cat, one that would produce show kittens she could keep or sell. None of these women made money breeding cats—they were lucky if they broke even after paying stud fees and veterinary bills, and the society meetings were more an occasion to gossip about human than feline affairs: infidelity, illness, misfortune, those staples of the coffee klatch.

In fact, when my grandmother was accepted as a member, she was made to understand that the Sunday afternoon meetings required coffee, not tea, and so her collection of Royal Crown Derby, Royal Worcester, and Spode tea services was never used or admired. The cups, some of them, were deep enough for coffee, but the matching pots were left in the cupboard in favor of a new fifty-cup electric percolator. A stainless-steel urn with a flat lid the size of a dinner plate and a basket for grounds big enough to use as a colander, the percolator was perhaps the ugliest thing in our house, and my grandmother loved it, representing, as it did, her membership in the Society.

When meetings were held at our house, it was my job to fill the percolator basket with rounded tablespoons of Chock Full o'Nuts ground coffee, each one lifted carefully from the can, a chore I guarded as an honor, despite the fact that I always lost count and had to start over, usually more than once. Nine years old, I was impressed by the meetings because, like Christmas, they required hired help, good china, the Chinese silver tray engraved with a dragon, and cakes from Paris Pastry. All the members were either thin or fat, one so thin she required an extra cushion on her chair, two so fat they had to be steered—"Politely! Politely!"—toward appropriate seats, the more spindly antiques hidden upstairs.

Before they sat, some of the members opened their purses and withdrew plastic sandwich bags filled with cat hair, wads of it combed from their animals. They gave this "wool," as my grandmother called it, to one of the society members, a peculiarly colorless little woman who spun the cat fur into yarn, using a handheld spindle. For a price, she would knit caps, scarves, even sweaters from this yarn, offering die-hard cat fanciers the opportunity to wear garments made from their own cats' fur. The spinster kept a black marker in her purse and made notations on the bags of fur, to keep them from getting mixed up, as all the combings looked alike, intermingled white and gray and brown hairs. The undyed knitwear she turned out was smog colored; like angora, it had a tendency to shed bits of fur into the atmosphere, making eyes and noses itch. I watched her at the meetings, spinning wool in her lap while the other women talked and ate. If she sat in a beam of sun, car hair floated in the air around her, settling onto the surface of her untouched coffee.

In June of 1970, my grandmother initiated a correspondence with the august S. M. Harding and began making arrangements to purchase a kitten. From a litter born in August, she selected a female, which would be shipped the following December, when the kitten was four months old and strong enough for an overseas flight. A week before Christmas, on an overcast and nearly Yule-like afternoon, we drove the endless Century Boulevard to LAX's international terminal to retrieve the animal, a scrap of a kitten that cost two hundred dollars, not including shipping, pedigree, veterinary certificate, and the equivalent of 5.17.6 pounds sterling for a molded plastic carrier with a wire mesh door against which the kitten had bumped and bloodied her nose during the twelve-hour flight. The total came to nearly three hundred dollars, an amount that, in 1970, seemed substantial enough to predict great things for "Tomita," this being the name inscribed on the carrier tag, a name that evoked hot blood and dark pigment, a feline flamenco.

But Tomita was a Lilac Point, white with the palest mauve-gray nose, ears, paws, and tail, her eyes the color ice acquires with sufficient depth. Himalayans are supposed to be "cobby," with short legs and thick, compact bodies, but at four months Tomita was as attenuated as one of her Siamese ancestors, and so skinny that her long fur couldn't hide her ribs. In a letter accompanying the cat, Mrs. Harding suggested that even if she didn't fill out, my grandmother could be confident that inside Tomita was a blueprint for perfection. All my grandmother had to do was select the right stud, one whose pedigree would override Tomita's flaws and call forth the expression of her potential.

So much for magic spells. Each night, under the standing lamp's glare, my grandmother sat in the corner of the sofa, again trying to read Mrs. Harding's chapters on dominant and recessive traits, drowsing with boredom and narcoleptic anxiety. Her head dropped forward onto her chest and then snapped up. The kitten batted at the pages and ran up and down the sofa back, pausing to sharpen her claws.

Long before she contemplated breeding cats, my grandmother's hypochondria had found its fullest expression in gynecological mishaps. To illustrate this, my mother used to tell altogether too many people the story of "the infamous tampon." When my grandmother was sixty-one, she'd had a small cyst removed from her vaginal wall. She begged to be hospitalized but, shamed by her doctor's insufficiently disguised amusement, agreed to an outpatient procedure, one accomplished with a local anesthetic and a lot of Miltown—a tranquilizer whose popularity preceded that of Valium, and which, as a child, I thought of in geographic terms: Mill Town, whose towering wheel steadily turned water to produce a sedating sound that inspired in its inhabitants a preternatural calm.

After the very minor surgery was accomplished, the doctor inserted a tampon to stanch what (if any) bleeding might occur. Assuming there were no complications, my grandmother wouldn't have to return to his office for another month.

But there was a complication: she couldn't remove the tampon. It had disappeared, she insisted, it was gone.

"Just feel for the string," my mother told her, seventeen years old and pregnant with me, her expectant middle announcing an inappropriate worldliness.

But my grandmother, weeping and shivering with fright, took a taxi back to the doctor's office and waited until the surgeon took the cotton plug out himself.

"Can you believe it!" my mother would say, years later. "I mean, can you!"

Whoever her audience was, that person laughed too hard to answer. Eavesdropping, taking advantage of the presumed incomprehension accorded children and servants, I tried to picture it: something that recalled an ancient illustration of hysteria, Plato's conceit of the untethered womb that floated like a balloon, higher and higher, dangling the lost tampon string and bumping up against my grandmother's liver and lungs.

Tomita went in and out of heat while my grandmother searched for the right stud, reading ads in the back of *Cat Fancy* magazine, calling breeders as far away as San Diego and Sacramento. The cat yowled, she rolled on the floor, she corkscrewed up and down the carpeted stairs, mad with unrequited lust. She peed on the beds and the chairs and on the navy blue jacket a guest left on one of the chairs. She succumbed to desperate, false pregnancies and dragged small plush toys under the beds, licking them until they were sodden with her pungent saliva. The veterinarian suggested that, were she not mated immediately, the cat should be spayed, these were the only humane options. And so my grandmother settled on a Seal Point owned by Crystal Penrose of Anaheim. The cat's name was Sir Galahad. Chivalrously, he raped Tomita for three consecutive days and delivered her from her torment.

Fresh lamb kidneys from the butcher, shrimp from the fishmonger dusted with powdered feline prenatal supplements, Nutra-Cal, Linatone, halibut liver oil imported from Morrell & Howells (a Richmond, Surrey, chemist recommended by S. M. Harding): for sixty-five days Tomita gestated, and at last produced a litter of one grotesquely large kitten that took six hours to deliver. At the end of what my grandmother, without irony, called her "confinement," the cat clawed her way across my bedroom rug, trying to escape her hindquarters and leaving a trail of blood and mucus that ended, abruptly, with the appearance of a shining purple something the size and shape of a big mango. Tomita ran under my bed, and my grandmother fell into a chair and screamed as I prodded the sinister, glistening mass, kitten and placenta both covered with lint and carpet hair. Having announced my intention to become a veterinarian, I didn't betray the fear and revulsion I felt. Neither did I do anything useful. The kitten fought his own way out of the amniotic sac.

We called him Mr. Boy, and, despite her initial, inauspicious response to him, his mother loved him with a devotion in proportion to the suffering she'd endured on his account. No place was safe enough to keep him: the scruff of Mr. Boy's neck was bald from having been dragged from closet to drawer to cupboard and back. All night, we heard his cries as he bumped, blind and deaf, over doorsills and down stairs. By twelve weeks, enormous eyes open, ears pricked, he outweighed his wasted mother. Like his father, he was dark, a Seal Point, and this pigment enhanced his Lothario aspect as he nursed, pinning Tomita's little body down with his front paws as he went from one to another of her raw pink teats, determined to have whatever was left of her.

"He has to go," my grandmother said. "They have to be separated." Mr. Boy was beautiful, but he wasn't show material; his ears were too big, and my grandmother ended up giving him to her hairdresser, Helga, a large and, as it turned out, unstable German woman, who fed Mr. Boy pâté until he died an early death, leaving the big woman so bereft that my grandmother had to find a new salon. Every week, when she drove to Robinson's in Beverly Hills to have her hair washed and set, Helga wept so that she couldn't concentrate. She rinsed my grandmother's hair the wrong color, she left permanent wave solution in for too long.

Dosed with double portions of halibut liver oil, brewer's yeast, and Nutra-Cal, Tomita regained her health and her lust. Undeterred by her traumatic first birth, she flung herself at people and furniture, rubbing her furry genitals on any available leg, animate or upholstered. Shunned by the other cats, she developed a hoarse, pleading cry, frightening even if you knew its source. My grandmother recovered from her anxiety enough to select a second "husband," as she called Sebastian, a bona fide Harding stud owned by a breeder in Pasadena.

As the pregnancy progressed, my grandmother comforted herself with the idea that Mr. Boy had been a useful first effort, so large that he had cleared the way for whatever might come. Still, she asked the vet if perhaps he wouldn't, after the sixtieth day, allow Tomita to stay at the animal clinic until the kittens arrived.

"You don't want to do that to her," he said, latching the door to her carrier. "The clinic is for sick animals. She's perfectly healthy." He looked at me. "You'll help your grandmother, won't you?"

I nodded.

"Can you?" she asked in the car on the way home. "Are you sure?"

I reminded her what everyone had said for the past weeks: cats had kittens without attendants.

"But what if she doesn't take care of them? Like with Mr. Boy?"

"She will. And if she doesn't, I can always wash them, I can cut the cords."

"Will you?"

I said I would.

The second delivery began as did the first, with Tomita's becoming abruptly agitated. She jumped down from where she'd been sleeping, on my bed, and I woke up. It was six in the morning, barely light. The cat, after a trip to the litter box, lay down on the old towel lining the bottom drawer of my dresser, the heavy drawer she'd learned to open herself, using what must have been superfeline powers to hook her paw through its handle and pull until the drawer slid out. On top of the dresser were the contents of my manicure kit, sterilized with rubbing alcohol and protected by a clean cloth. The curved scissors were too small, but they were sharp, the closest I had to anything that might be considered surgical.

I sat down on my knees, deciding not to wake up my grandmother. She'd be surprised, and proud of me, when I came down to breakfast to announce that it was all over and everything was fine. And after the enormous Mr. Boy, labor did go fast, a first kitten appeared within minutes, and Tomita left nothing for me to do. She stripped off the sac with her teeth, licked the kitten clean, chewed and swallowed the afterbirth as the kitten began rooting for a nipple.

Then a second came, delivered without a cry. But after tearing off the sac, Tomita didn't lick it. She pushed it away with her nose. I laid the kitten next to her and she got up, she put her body between it and the first.

"Come on," I said. "Clean him up." I considered going upstairs to wake my grandmother, but decided against it. The vet's office wasn't open yet, and this wasn't an emergency. I took the cloth from the top of the dresser and soaked it with warm water from my bathroom tap, washed the little white face, so enigmatic with its sealed eyes and ears, its whiskers aligned in three rows, tidy, perfect. But there was something odd about the umbilical cord; while the first kitten's had been straight, this one's was fantastically looped and tangled. I chose one and then another place to slip the curved blades of my polished scissors, but then found I couldn't bring myself to close them. I didn't know where to cut it.

The kitten lay on my washed hand, showing me the minute pads of its paws, their translucent tiny claws. Tomita's disinterest was so absolute, I knew this baby was mine, imagined the bottle required to feed it, a doll bottle; I must have one somewhere. But first I had to cut the cord. I couldn't be squeamish—crazy—like my grandmother. An inch from the body, that was the rule, and I tried to follow it. I nudged one blade of the scissors into a loop about that distance from the little pink abdomen, its dusting of white fuzz.

Immediately I knew the mistake I'd made, was sick with the shock of it. Blood spurted with the beat of the kitten's heart, a first long arc, then shorter, shorter, then only a trickle. I had to stop the flow, but how? I couldn't keep my finger on the place—the wound I had made—the kitten fought me off. For a second it did. How I wished, decades later, that I could forget the feel of its first ardent kick, the tiny claws on my wrist, and how quickly it weakened and failed. In my hands the little body beneath the fine white fur faded from pink to mauve to gray. Blood ran down my arm and dripped from my elbow onto the towel, the carpet, my nightgown.

Looped, not straight. The coils had looked like what they were: intestines. Textbook perfect, but I hadn't understood. I'd been fooled by their having been misplaced.

I rocked on my heels and held the kitten against the warmth of my chest. No no no, I kept talking to it as I paced in circles around my room, the hall.

In the bathroom, I laid it very carefully in the smooth bowl of the sink, while, on my knees, I tried to throw up.

Back in the bedroom, the cat looked at me with her ice blue eyes. I didn't dare put the dead kitten next to her. And I didn't hide it from my grandmother, didn't bury it and pretend it hadn't been born. Pretend that once again, Tomita had had a single kitten. How easy that would have been— why didn't I?

I skipped school and drove with my grandmother to the animal hospital, the kitten's corpse on my lap, swaddled in a fresh towel.

"It wouldn't have lived," the vet said.

I told him what I hadn't said to my grandmother, explaining what I'd done, the pink loop, the scissors. "I killed it," I said. By now I had cried so long that the unwrapped bundle on the stainless steel examining table looked blurry, unreal, like one of the old stuffed animals Tomita had dragged under my bed.

"No," he said. "Not you."

"Who?" I managed after a silence.

He shrugged. "It would have died anyway."

"You could have operated on it. Put them back in."

He shook his head. "That kind of surgery, on a new kitten. It wouldn't have lived."

"But at least we would have been trying."

"There was something very wrong with it. That's why the mother wouldn't touch it. She knew."

I shook my head. "But before I—it wasn't dead. It was alive."

He put his hand on my sleeve and I pulled away. "I wouldn't have performed that surgery. I would have suggested euthanizing the kitten."

I nodded. *That would have been you,* I thought. *Not me.* A slender needle, a way of going to sleep.

At night, Tomita crouched at the head of my bed and licked my temples with her punishing tongue. Unaccountably, the same devotion she'd given Mr. Boy, undiluted and monomaniacal, she transferred now to me, and for my company she left her remaining kitten mewing in the drawer, hungry and complaining stridently. I made a nest for it by my pillow, using one of my flannel nightgowns, and in the dark I listened to the noises of its suckling. Unless I left my hand on Tomita's head, unless I stroked her, the cat would stand up and shake the kitten off.

How much blood? A cup's worth? And how to give it back? I couldn't bring myself to make a deep enough cut, and nosebleeds didn't count; they were cheating. It had to be the nail scissors, the same bright murdering blade. How many scratches, how many pricks? When I got up, the cat followed me into the bathroom. Sometimes she left the kitten, sometimes she brought it along, sat watching me with it swinging from her jaws.

"Too highly strung," my grandmother decided. She retired Tomita, had her spayed, and bought another breeder from S. M. Harding, a Chocolate Point named Jessica, whose estral cycles were comparatively demure, and who mated without incident. On day sixty of gestation, my grandmother packed the new cat into a carrier and dropped her off at the vet's. Six kittens each time, big litters, no complications.

Years passed, and we never spoke about what happened with the scissors. Not directly. But I did tell my grandmother I no longer planned to be a vet. We were washing cups after one of the yearly Himalayan Society meetings. I'd measured the coffee, and for the members I'd done as my grandmother asked, I'd demonstrated how Tomita came when I whistled, how she sat on her haunches and begged.

The usually silent spinster put down her spindle and yarn to clap. "Just like a dog!" she said approvingly, and after they all went home, my grandmother told me again what a good veterinarian I was going to be.

"I don't want to be a vet."

"Well, why not!"

"I just don't."

"I think that's a shame."

I shrugged.

"You're so calm," she went on. "You have what it takes."

"What's that?" I asked, taking another cup to dry.

"Nerves of steel."

BEACH TRIP

A trip to the beach: we'd arrive at one and leave by four, but still, it's an occasion for which we have to pack. Into the trunk of the car my grandfather loads a card table and four folding chairs; a huge striped canvas umbrella; full changes of clothes for each of us—my grandparents, my mother, and me; a transistor radio; binoculars; straw hats; terry cloth robes; towels. And lunch: sandwiches, salads, Thermos hot and Thermos cold, cookies and fruit.

It takes half an hour to carry and assemble our camp on the shore. When we're through, we sit perspiring in our chairs, conspicuous among all the hippies who, in 1969, make a point of having nothing. My mother, if she deigns to accompany us, spreads her towel some distance away and sleeps through lunch. When I'm not swimming I sit on the sand at her head and, reaching carefully around her dark hair, make her a crown of seashells: Lady Slippers placed bottom side up so that their blush undersurfaces show, limpets with spokes of color—white, blue, lavender—and in the center, if I'm lucky enough to find one, a sea urchin laced with green and pink. When it's cloudy, she turns over on her stomach and pulls her arms tight in to her sides, digs her toes into the sand, seeking the heat of its deeper layers. Later, when we're going to bed, she'll be putting on her suede jacket with the eight-inch fringe on its sleeves, dressing to go out.

With his binoculars, my grandfather tracks my progress into the water, not relying on lifeguards who are, he thinks, entrusted with too many lives to save. My grandmother watches for fat people. Obsessed with corpulence—an *idée fixe,* she admits it—she gets an almost illicit thrill from the sight of copious and nearly naked flesh trudging thunderously up the sand. Men are not without interest, but it's the fat women for whom she yearns. And she is brazen; sometimes she stands up to get a better view.

"Look! Look! Look at that one!" she'll cry as a monumental woman approaches, the fat on her hips moving with tidal force, breaking over knees and elbows. *"Look,"* my grandmother hisses, engrossed, appalled, delighted. She speaks in a stage whisper—this is the extent of her discretion, what she can manage under the circumstances. Besides, she relies on her own special language of fat, untranslatable by strangers. "Look at that *halem!*"

In Shanghai, in 1910, the Halems, a family of Jews, changed their name to Bottomly as part of their campaign of assimilation into the British Concession. This is the etymology for my grandmother's code word for derriere. "Let's go look at the *halems,*" she says, when suggesting a beach trip.

Is it because she weighs only ninety pounds that fat women excite her imagination? *Fatsalagas,* she calls them— this is a word of her own coinage—or *sights.* "Let's go *sight* seeing."

"How much, Bunny?" she asks my grandfather. (She calls him by this name because of his emotional investment in his vegetable garden.) "How much? What do you think?"

My grandfather, who knows it is pointless to discourage her, turns to look. "Three-fifty," he says. "Maybe four." Each time, she insists that he guess the poundage. She won't stop asking until he complies.

Next to them, my mother sleeps with a resolve she doesn't waste on nonescapist pursuits. I chew my sandwich for its taste, spitting as much as I can stand to part with into a hole I've dug for the purpose, turning my back to the other families, the normal ones. I don't have to hide from mine, involved as they are in their own interests. In another twenty minutes I can go back into the water.

"Now how about that!" Squeezing my grandfather's hand with a glee bordering on hysteria, she's found another.

"Steady," my grandfather says. "Keep your hair on." Once—only once, but still—she tipped over backward in her chair.

"That arm! It would take four of my legs to make an arm like that!"

How many of her buttocks would add up to one of theirs? How many times would she have to multiply her tiny breasts to fill a single bra cup of their bathing suits? These calculations, the mathematics of fat, are essential to her enjoyment.

"Now, Bunny, I mean it! Eight? Ten?" She points at a woman emerging from the rest rooms, wearing a vast muumuu. How many dresses, my grandmother wants to know, could she get from the fabric of that tentlike garment?

"I can't see," my grandfather says.

"Yes, you can. You can."

"Eight."

"Only eight?"

"All right, then. Ten."

She nods, satisfied, scanning the sands, the surf, the parking lot.

"I'm going back in the water," I say, and my grandfather nods. He holds out his hand to my grandmother.

"I need them now," he says, taking hold of the binoculars.

THE SUPERMARKET
DETECTIVE

I was a shoplifter when I was thirteen years old. Not an occasional or casual thief, I stole ritualistically: on the same day
each week, from the same store, with the same partner.

I spent many Friday nights at Diane's, where we ran up
the driveway from the school bus, dropped our books on her
bed, and changed from our gray and blue school uniforms
into our shoplifting gear: voluminous army-surplus coats
with dozens of pockets and two linings. We'd walk the mile
to the strip mall giddy with anticipation, stopping en route at
an abandoned building site, behind which we slipped and
slid down a dry, grassy embankment to search through the
trash at the bottom of the gulch. Someone—who?—left
pornography there. Dirty, torn pictures of women, very
young women, pictured alone, their slender purple throats
garroted with cords, or together with one, two, even three
partners. We studied these pictures silently—this is what
happens to bad girls—making no comment to each other.
Sometimes we buried them.

A few blocks away we shoplifted at Pic 'N' Save, a cut-rate remainder outlet: costume jewelry and makeup, false eyelashes—little things slipped into a wide sleeve. After perfecting our technique, we graduated to belts, skirts, blouses, dresses. Each haul had to be better and more daring than the last. And each time we stole, we bought one thing, using the little bag with the receipt stapled to it as a disguise, one we depended on to protect us from being perceived as thieves as we moved carefully past the register. To ensure that the bracelets and rings and sunglasses didn't clank together and announce their presence in our jacket linings, we had to move much more slowly than we wanted. Perhaps the disguise worked, because we weren't caught. Not then, anyway.

At Diane's house there was a small unused bedroom off the kitchen, and we hung our stolen clothes in its closets, put the underwear and jewelry in the drawers, set the wigs on stands before the vanity mirror. It was impossible for me to take any of my shoplifted things home to my grandparents, but Diane's mother and father were immersed in Eastern philosophy to the point of benign vagueness. Her father, an internist, was one of the few to practice acupuncture in the seventies. On weekends he and her mother went to the Self-Realization Fellowship Center, founded in 1925 by Paramhansa Yogananda, an Indian mystic. Diane's parents, who were born in Germany, before the war, were quintessential Southern Californians—attractive, hip seekers—and they never seemed to notice our growing collection of stolen clothes, which included, for each of us, vinyl wallets filled with false identification. Not the kind of fake ID offered in the backs of magazines, not the kind that looked remotely plausible, these were little cards we made ourselves. For hours we hunched over Diane's desk, drawing tiny self-portraits which we Scotch taped onto cards bearing invented names and addresses. We made wallet "photographs" of pretend boyfriends, pictures that would not have fooled even the most myopic. But that didn't matter; we were drawing them for ourselves, no one else, props for a fantasy life that included romance as well as freedom.

The next day, Saturday, we would each pack a small suitcase (of exclusively stolen items—that was the rule) and walk to the Texaco station near Diane's house. In the dirty rest room, flies crawling on the window, we changed our clothes, and our personalities. What we put on was overtly sexual: halter tops, high platform shoes. A lot of makeup and perfume. When we wore our "costumes" on Halloween that year, my grandmother took one look at us and said, "What are you supposed to be? Prostitutes at Hollywood and Vine?"

Diane and I looked at each other, astonished. Was that how we appeared? Was that what we had intended?

Unrecognizable, even to each other, we'd call a cab from the gas station pay phone, and then we did go to Hollywood, where we discovered that we had lost even our youth, and that we could be served in bars, without showing ID. Not knowing any better, we drank sickening liqueurs like Galliano and made brazen conversation with strangers, using lines cribbed from late-show movies. We let those strangers buy us drinks. And nothing very bad ever happened to us— though it might have quite easily: we were young, we knew nothing of men, we had no money beyond cab fare.

Once, when a man made a pass at me, Diane told him I was taken, I had a boyfriend. "Show him," she said, and I shook my head.

"Come on," she egged. I took out my wallet and opened it. The man looked at the tiny drawing covered with layers of Scotch tape and further obscured by the wallet's clouded plastic window. "Tell him your boyfriend's name," Diane said. She was aggressive when disguised.

But I kept my eyes down, on the bar, I didn't say anything, and the man went away.

"Pinch and Save," my mother rechristened Pic 'N' Save. She didn't care that I shoplifted; she thought it was funny. Expecting to shock her, I'd confessed the source of all the junky jewelry and clothes, but it hadn't worked; she betrayed no disapproval. Of course, my season of stealing must have been over, if I was talking about it with my mother. I must have been ready to stop, at least for a while.

The next time I took something from a store—the time I was caught—I was out of practice. It had been years, and I no longer saw much of Diane, our friendship a casualty of anorexia. I'd lost her when I lost weight, unwittingly disrupting what had been a critical balance: she'd been the slender one; I'd been the smart one.

I still remember the feeling of the store detective's hand on my arm in the parking lot. And I remember how hot it was, July in the San Fernando Valley; even at ten at night I could feel the heat of the asphalt burning through the slender soles of my shoes. I was seventeen, a couple of months away from going to college. Here's what I stole: a pink box of Correctol laxative, thirty candy-coated pink tablets that I planned to take all at once. They'd make me sick, and that was the plan.

Correct All. That was what I wanted from the pills, which cost only a few dollars, money I had, but I couldn't pay for them because I couldn't enter into a transaction that might reveal my secret, sordid, and pathetic life to a grocery checker. So I hid them under my shirt.

Ralph's Supermarket detective escorted me forcibly into an office behind a two-way mirror and called the phone number I gave him. My grandparents arrived within minutes, wearing pajamas under overcoats. My grandmother took one look at me and said, "What has she done?" Always ready to believe the worst about anyone, she was a woman disappointed by unrelieved virtue.

But my grandfather, who was eighty-eight at the time and had high blood pressure, attacked the store detective in his little office behind the bakery department. "She did not do it!" he said, throwing aside the pink box that the man had taken from me in the parking lot. My grandfather's face went the dangerous purple color that usually presaged a nosebleed, and he stood up straight and poked the store detective in the chest with his finger. "Don't you understand?" he said. "She is incapable of dishonesty!"

How awful to be defended in guilt, so much more painful than my grandmother's correct, if insulting, assumptions. I folded my arms in front of my chest; through the mirror I watched a young woman in a pink smock tie string around a box of cookies and hand it across the bakery counter.

"Then why did I catch her in the parking lot with merchandise she didn't pay for?" the detective asked.

My grandfather swatted the air. "You made a mistake," he said.

The detective shook his head.

"She is going to Stanford University!" My grandfather made this announcement as if he were providing a key character witness, as he believed he was.

The detective smiled nastily. "Well," he said. "I'm sure *Stanford University* doesn't knowingly admit criminals. Maybe I should send them a letter."

I said nothing, trying not to look at the little box on his desk, hoping no one would discern the awful secret beneath the incidental crime: I was hungry; I'd lost my talent for starving. This seemed to me as awful as the possibility of a letter sent to school ahead of me to proclaim me a thief.

Remanded to my grandparents, issued a warning that any subsequent theft would be prosecuted, I followed them to the car.

"What was that you stole?" my grandmother asked, curious.

"Tampons," I said with my back to her, trying to fit my bike into the trunk.

She nodded. This made sense. Any reasonable person would of course be tempted to steal something so embarrassing.

I embellished the lie. "The checkers were all boys," I told her.

"What?" My grandfather cupped his hand around his good ear. "What?"

"Nothing, Bunny. Nothing." She reached over the backseat to hand me the keys.

"I'm sorry you had to drive in the dark," I said, backing out of the space.

When we got home, my mother's car was in the driveway, and she was pacing in the hall, wild-eyed. "I called to say good night. No one answered. I called five times."

She held up her hand, wiggling her fingers. "Five. So I drove all the way over here." She looked at me, at her parents in their coats and pajamas. "What on earth are you all doing?"

My grandfather shook his head. "I can't hear you," he said, and started up the stairs.

"Nothing," I said.

She turned to her mother. "Nothing?" she demanded.

My grandmother leaned toward her. "Female trouble," she said, in her loudest stage whisper.

A Pilgrimage to
Saks Fifth Avenue

At five, my daughter had a clear understanding of how she wanted to look, of her *style,* and as the clothes we bought together reflected her taste, her early-morning exercise of laying out a day's outfits was one she enjoyed. If she lingered over her choices, if she matched several different sets of blouses and skirts and tights, it wasn't out of confusion but to prolong a pleasure.

At seventeen, a freshman in college, before I went to bed I would lay out clothes for class the next morning. Having worn a uniform for the previous fifteen years—each day a white blouse, gray skirt, blue blazer, and saddle shoes—I hadn't had sufficient practice getting dressed in clothes that were supposed to announce who I was. Preppy? Hippie? Nerd? That was complicated enough without factoring in gender. Just how much of a female did I want to appear? I could waste whole minutes in the contemplation of one button on a sweater: done? undone?

In the dormitory, working in the cramped glare of a Tensor reading lamp, I opened and closed drawers quietly so as not to wake my roommate and be discovered in such foolish disorder. For as long as an hour or two, I'd lay tops to bottoms, considering every possible combination, often only to reject them all in favor of sweatpants or army-surplus fatigues, the fallback of a moth-eaten black pullover. I never wore most of the clothes purchased for college—sweater sets and pleated trousers still bearing their price tags, a dirndl skirt and a kilt, ribbed tights, the one *de rigueur* pair of Levi's 501s—because in all of them I knew I would feel conspicuous. Even slipping on the shiny penny loafers, bright coins tucked into their slots, I was ill at ease, as if I anticipated being caught impersonating the classic coed, that emblematic girl for whom the school wardrobe had been selected. It was only in my faded, frayed army pants and black pullover that I believed I disappeared, except for my head and my note-taking hands, all that classes required. In effect, I'd assembled a new school uniform, aggressively unfashionable, lest anyone mistake me for someone who cared about such vulgar superficialities.

So why on weekends did I go by myself to department stores, to Saks and Bullocks and I. Magnin's and Bonwit's—the same stores in which my mother shopped—and try on clothes for hours, compulsively pulling on and tearing off hundreds of garments, time disappearing as it does when one is under a narcotic influence? If I never bought anything, it was because not one sweater or dress or pair of pants ever announced itself as *me*. At least not a me I was able to recognize.

Hadn't enough hours of my life already been squandered in dressing rooms? Hadn't I sat for too long already on the seat built into the corner formed by two white walls, waiting for my mother's shadow to fall across the slats of the swinging door, warning me of her return from the frontier of the clothing racks? Those doors, which snapped at my fingers lingering on the doorjamb, reminded me of saloon doors in a Saturday morning cartoon, the ones a gunslinger bursts through before he opens fire. Their slats offered a sliced version of life beyond them and made me feel naked. Whenever anyone passed—another customer or a sales lady with eyeglasses hung around her neck on a chain—I took a deep breath and sucked in my stomach.

Whatever my mother brought back for me was too small. I could have told her so, but she made me try on everything before her wincing eyes. She had to see that the zipper tab was stopped in mid-ascent by the flesh of my stomach, the puffed sleeve arrested in its climb up my arm, the pants stuck just below the emphatic presence of my bottom. This was our weekend drama; this was what had to be rehearsed over and over: I did not fit, could not be crammed, into the space she made for me in her life.

Years passed, college ended, but I didn't outgrow these isolated pilgrimages; I returned to them during periods of psychic strain. In the last months of my mother's life, several times a week I'd wait for the visiting nurse to release me from her bedside; then I'd head for the Galleria. Alone, in one sterile dressing room after another I watched myself disrobe in the mirror, then dressed and dressed and dressed again while, less than a mile away, my mother slept, her face erased of expression by morphine.

What was it, still, about shopping, a skill so simple that I knew of no one else who had failed to master it? Why was it impossible to find clothes that I could recognize as *me* with the kind of confidence my daughter had in kindergarten? It wasn't a matter of looking pretty or *au courant*. For me, the stakes were higher than those, locked as I was in an argument I couldn't win and couldn't walk out on—the one with my mother, invisible but just as surely present in the dressing room as she was when I was five, her impatient hands zipping me tight, caught and squirming, into yet another Florence Eismann jumper.

"A free spirit," she used to call me, her tone making it clear that this wasn't a compliment. Neither was it true, for standing defiant before her, rumpled and scowling, elbows torn, plackets frayed, ink stained, who was I other than Not Her, improbably cool and unwrinkled by the end of a day, always dressed as if she had more money than she did, while I dressed as if I had less?

Fifteen and newly thin, I'd had a clarity I now lacked: a first rule of fashion—Black—and a second: Whatever it is, if it makes you look thinner, buy it. This was a good apprenticeship for adulthood in New York, but in California, circa 1976, I was a freak. "She's gone into mourning," my grandmother would announce to visitors, trying to explain my anomalous mien to sunny L.A. suburbanites. "We don't know why," she'd add disingenuously, washing her hands of the matter.

I stood, silent and scowling, looked no one in the eye, and offered a hand as cool and inanimate as that of a corpse. One day the alchemy of will and desire would allow me to peel the soul from my bones, unstick mind from brain, and hasten my ectoplasmic flight from all the inconveniences and humiliations of flesh. Until then, my body, like a botched magic act—the girl who didn't disappear—was to be ignored and draped. Shoved offstage.

Cursed with a strong constitution, I remained stubbornly incarnate only to discover that my specialty among the seven deadly sins was pride. Here was the tortured El Greco figure I had made, not the one I was given, but the one for which I'd suffered, a silhouette that proved the strength of my determination, the subjugation of appetite, curves planed to angles, arms to sticks. And what about those collarbones I had excavated, the waist I had pared down? How wrong would it be to reveal them?

College offered opportunities to reinvent myself away from my mother's critical gaze, but I lacked grace, or the ability to forgive—whatever it was that might have allowed me to start from scratch. Instead, I determined to form myself in opposition to Her, to all the many hers. To her at, say, twenty-five, when I was seven and she the unattainable object of my desire, the focus of every wild longing, with her picture hats and pastel dresses, sling-back shoes, painted toenails. Or to her at thirty, wearing wet-look boots, a jacket with a fringe. Or thirty-five, all grown-up and businesslike, a two-piece suit, cream silk blouse, Charles Jourdan pumps. I watched carefully as, over the years, she covered choice sartorial territories, leaving me trekking belligerently through wildernesses of thrift stores and army-surplus outlets. Handbags? I replaced them with an unwieldy satchel, taking it to lunches, dinners, parties, feeling its weight dragging one shoulder down. Pink? I never touched the stuff. Matching separates? I went for clashing.

Sometimes I was thin, and sometimes I wasn't, and the clothes I wore betrayed as little consistency as the body under them. Beaded sweaters, pedal pushers, parachute pants, cropped toreador jackets, any style so dated or wacky that I'd never seen my mother wear it—whatever, in fact, she was sure to consider dowdy or peculiar: black coolie slippers and Mao jackets, bowling shoes, threadbare tweed sports coats with their sleeves rolled up to the biceps. Each break, I came home determined to provoke those same cool looks of dismay I'd once feared. If I wore anything she bought for me it was in a purposefully inappropriate context, once walking across campus in the archetypal Lanz flannel nightgown sorority girls wore—to bed.

And yet, the spell of those department store dressing rooms: women on either side of me, often in pairs, the intimate choreography of their four feet, red toenail polish showing through nude stockings. They talked as I sat on the little upholstered bench, my arms crossed defensively, eavesdropping as they assessed each garment, as they picked and they chose. Sometimes it was a mother and a grown-up daughter in the little room next to mine. Transfixed, I listened to their voices, laughter, sighs. How easily I could see them: a woman of fifty, the freckled backs of her hands, the wedding band that no longer slid past the knuckle, and the daughter, head bent forward as her mother's fingers coaxed a hook into a tiny eye.

"What do you think, Mom?"

"You can do better," the older voice replied.

And what about me, couldn't I do better? Often, my underwear, with its failing elastic, was so old that I could use the only rule of dress my grandmother had ever passed on— advice dating back to button-up undergarments. "If your knickers fall off," she announced, apropos of nothing—I think we were eating lunch in a cafe—"don't pick them up, dear. Just keep walking."

Thirty years old, married, a mother, I undertook a program of reformation, one accomplished with modest results. I upgraded my underwear to the point that I could feel confident if run over and subsequently stripped by an EMT.

But forget hats. I'll never be able to carry one off. Even the ones that look good. Every few years I buy one and try to develop a hat persona, but it doesn't take. It must be a talent like that for sunglasses, which I purchase and then immediately lose, sit on, break. Hats and sunglasses: these are the hardest because my mother was never without them, looking great and knowing it, very Jackie O. As my stances have tended to be, historically, self-conscious and symbolic, to my mother's funeral I did wear a hat—one I bought for the occasion, black with a chin-length veil. A dramatic gesture, but at twenty-four I'd yet to master subtlety. To exorcise this unfortunate accessory, packed away like a relic in tissue paper for all the intervening years, I loaned it to my daughter for her second-grade play. Hats can be rehabilitated; I, however, remain my mother's daughter.

Approaching the same age as my mother when she died, along with laugh lines I've developed a small, haggard pucker where jaw meets neck. I recognize this slackening as hers—our throats are aging in the same way, at the same time—and the new flaw has instructed me. Surprisingly, I'm not resentful of this echo: not only is it another of the lines of unanticipated dialogue between the living and the dead, but it's awakened me to a vanity I didn't know I possessed. Only in cataloguing its deterioration have I discovered my affection for my neck. It turned out better than I expected it would at eleven or twelve, paralyzed before my reflection in the bathroom mirror, comparing what was still cloaked in baby fat with the long, elegant stalk that supported my mother's impeccably made-up face.

The rest of my body, too, clothed or unclothed, how like hers it is, fingers and toes, the same enviable waist and, despite the thousands of miles I've jogged, less than exemplary legs. I take my body—the one she gave me—to department stores, where I buy it things. I can do this if I have a goal, like a black crewneck sweater with three-quarter-length sleeves. The more specific the better, because too many choices tend to hypnotize, and I have suffered the occasional recidivist fugue, especially in Designer Sportswear, populated as it is with the sort of soignée fortyish women whose clothes announce, in my mother's voice, Smart, Versatile, Tailored, and many other things that have nothing to do with sports. I always go to Saks. Now that Bonwit's and Magnin's are gone, it is the last of her temples that remain, and I look forward to entering the ground floor of the store on Fifth Avenue, next door to Saint Patrick's Cathedral, whose power to return me to my essential, worshipful self is not nearly so strong.

The Saks on Fifth Avenue isn't the one we went to together, and yet it is: the shining floor and the sounds of hundreds of high heels striking it, the lit glass counters, warm to the touch; decorative boughs overhead, trimmed according to the season, with blossoms, leaves, or sparkling snow. I can't ever predict the effect of this environment. "It makes you nuts," a friend clarifies. But in different ways, at different times. Its potency is such that I only go there as a last stop; I make sure that there is no place I have to arrive afterward, other than home.

A long narrow skirt, charcoal gray. Six pairs of underpants. A tunic-length cashmere sweater. A pair of side-zippered trousers with narrow legs, no pleats or cuffs. A Little Black Dress. I've succeeded at all of these, assembled a new uniform no less sober than that I wore in grade school.

And I still try on clothes I have no intention of buying, my fits of pretend shopping sandwiched, once or twice a year, between appointments, that accidental hour, say, between the doctor's office and the editor's—between one kind of nakedness and another—a temporal blank onto which a question is inscribed: who am I, traveling from here to there? The ghostly reflection (a see-through me, not all there) in a shop window I pass can still be enough to provoke me into taking off my clothes behind a curtain, exchanging them for another set, and looking at the woman in the mirror. Corporeal, not ectoplasmic.

But these days the dressing room isn't in Saks. It's Andy's Chee-Pees or Reminiscence: downtown, grubby, *thrift*. The woman in the mirror tries on girls' clothes that she doesn't buy. Beaded sweaters and army pants and beat-up denim jackets. A glimpse of herself, hurrying across campus, head down, scowling in the sunshine.

Renewal

We're in the San Fernando Valley Department of Motor Vehicles, "home of the great unwashed," my mother calls it. Among the dozen or so people taking the written test required for a California driver's license, my grandmother strikes an even more original—eccentric—note than usual. But then I'm often surprised when I see her in a workaday context. Sitting at a battered school desk, she's wearing red lipstick and pearls, a hectic spot of unblended rouge on each cheekbone. Her permed curls are black, unnaturally so for a woman in her late seventies, her petite legs crossed, right over left, the top foot bouncing nervously up and down in its black suede sling-back pump. The lipstick, the jewelry, the dark pink suit with gold buttons: she's ridiculously overdressed for the DMV; everyone else is slouching in T-shirts and shorts. But a license renewal, involving as it does official forms and government employees, intimidates my grandmother, who lives in chronic, unjustified fear of losing her citizenship.

"Because I was born a Jew," she's clarified, ancestry being one of the inconveniences she feels she has overcome, at least internally. But, as she says, she can't change her face. She came to the United States in 1939, "through Mexico," she whispers dramatically, and she won't set foot across the southern border, sure that she wouldn't get back: someone would realize and rectify what must have been the mistake of letting her through. In terms of renewing a driver's license, the past conspires to make my grandmother frantic—enough to spend an hour titivating. *Titivate* is one of her favorite words.

The examination area desks are the type that fill college classrooms, each with a small writing surface attached to the chair arm. Some of the people taking the test can hardly fit into the seats and have crammed themselves in sideways, their flanks dented painfully by the laminate writing surfaces. But there's more than enough room for my grandmother. Five feet tall and ninety pounds, were it not for her aggressively painted lips and cheeks, she might appear as a wizened child. She waves at me in a manner intended to be subtle, undetectable by anyone but me, but even from my vantage in the waiting area, some ten yards away, I can see that she's not patting the curls behind her ear. I shake my head and avert my face, hoping to discourage her, but when I turn back she's not working on her test; she's waving openly to get my attention.

I look around for a proctor or an officer and, seeing no one monitoring the exam area, walk with determined casualness over to the white plastic chain cordoning off the desks.

"What is it?" I mouth.

"Number seventeen," she hisses.

"What?"

"Number seventeen!" The people around my grandmother look up from their desks to stare at her, at me. "You read it," she says, as if we are alone in the crowded room. "Explain it to me."

"I can't do that!"

"Yes, you can." She looks not so much aggrieved as puzzled by my refusal. "You can," she says again.

"No," I whisper, loudly enough for the other people to hear. "I'm not allowed to. It's a *test*." I duck under the plastic chain to get closer to my grandmother. I'm supposed to be here for moral support, which doesn't mean cheating, I am about to tell her, when she takes the whole test and shoves it, folded, into my hands. My head bent over her desk, both of us hidden by my curtain of long hair (a technique perfected in school, to get away with reading novels in class), I try to give the test back, but she avoids my hand by collapsing dramatically over the little writing surface. "Fix it!" she hisses.

"No!"

"Yes!"

"No!"

"YES!"

With the test clamped under my elbow and hidden by my hair, I duck back under the chain. The rest room line is long and it doesn't move. I give up on getting a stall, and, as I don't dare leave the building, go back to my plastic chair in the waiting area. Still relying on my hair to hide me, I bend over the test on my knees and read hurriedly through what's printed on the long narrow sheet of newsprint. She's missed about twenty of the thirty multiple-choice questions. I know because, even though I'm only fourteen and more than a year away from my first permit, I'm the one who's drilled her for the past few evenings, going page by page through the California drivers' manual. And I'm not surprised that she's answered so many of the questions incorrectly. Not only does she lack the discipline required for study, she's offended by the very idea of the test, one she's taken before and remembers as useless. How can they ask it of a woman who's been driving for decades, one who got her first driver's permit in Shanghai, at fifteen years of age?

It might be an apocryphal tale—and, more than sixty years later, even she might not remember the facts—but my grandmother has told me that the Shanghai driver's test included her navigating the Bund, a flock of sheep, a marketplace filled with peasants, two hairpin passes (there are no mountains in or around Shanghai), and further improbable trials. In Italy, however, she did drive her Hispana Suiza back and forth over the Alps, and she interrupted one of our evening drills to search for a photograph of the car. Black and highly polished, it had a long hood and a spare, chrome-spoked wheel displayed on the luggage compartment—"the boot," she called it. From the running board she smiled flirtatiously and touched the toe of her pointed shoe to the dusty road.

The apparent contradiction between my grandmother's anxiety over her license and her citizenship, and her willingness to risk getting caught cheating on the examination (which, one would assume, could endanger the very documents over which she obsessively worries), is just another of a fabric of paradoxes that together comprise her personality. She's reserved and she's bawdy; she's strict and she's indulgent; she's cowed by authority and eager to flout it—except with regard to money. She would never steal; she would never think of deceiving the IRS or defaulting on a payment. *Dun* is a word she speaks with excited horror.

When I look over at the test area, I see that she's taken some papers out of her handbag and spread them on the desk as camouflage. This ruse looks like what it is—a pile of grocery lists and old envelopes—but no one seems to notice. A female DMV clerk escorts a new test taker past my grandmother's desk. "Hello!" my grandmother greets the clerk, believing in the power of a strong offensive, and she waves at the uniformed woman, who glares at her and keeps walking. I wait until the clerk is behind the crowded counter, dealing with the next in line, before I duck back under the chain.

"Check it," I whisper.

"What about number seventeen?"

"Check all of them!"

"Why!"

"They're wrong!"

"Which one?"

"Lots of them! All of them!"

My grandmother pushes the test away and begins to cry. As I look around to see who might be watching—Can it be that no one is proctoring this exam?—she puts her pen in my hand, tweaks at the frayed edge of my cutoff shorts. "Please!" she whispers histrionically, and she adds volume to the previously silent weeping.

"*Stop it!*" I say, savage with nerves.

Back in my chair, I complete the test quickly. The hardest part is inflating my usually small and controlled check marks into ones like hers, with wild dramatic tails that skid off the page.

When I look out from under my hair to see if it's safe to return the test, I see the DMV clerk standing over my grandmother, who has dumped her whole handbag out on the little desktop, spilling lipsticked pink Kleenex and loose change on the floor around her.

"What are you doing here?" the clerk says as I crawl under the chain and begin picking up the coins and tissues. I return the folded test to my grandmother among the clutter, dumping all of it in her lap, and not answering the clerk because I'm mute with fear, so scared that black swaths press in from the periphery of my vision. Like curtains closing after a performance, they undulate and sway. I stand up and immediately squat back down, holding on to the chair back, too dizzy to stand.

"You're not allowed in here," the clerk says loudly, broadcasting to the people around us, all of whom are staring. "This is *the test area*."

"I was just helping my grandmother," I manage from the floor.

My grandmother looks at the clerk. "I fell in the bank last year," she says, inspired. She is telling the truth. "Broke my hip. Just this kind of slippery floor," she adds, pointing unnecessarily.

The clerk looks from me to my grandmother and back. "All right. All right," she says.

My grandmother retrieves the test from among the Kleenex in her lap and hands it to the woman, the cheap paper rumpled and even slightly torn, marred with dramatic cross-outs, some mine, some hers. The clerk's expression as she regards the sheet is complex, involving suspicion, exasperation, pity, exhaustion.

I take my grandmother's elbow with exaggerated tenderness, and we follow the officer, as I've come to regard the clerk, back to her place at the long counter where, having imagined every awful outcome, I wait for us to be apprehended, humiliated, *booked*. My grandmother, however, looks triumphant; she squeezes my hand and gives me a bright, girlish smile.

Using a printed key, the clerk goes over the test answers with a red pen, hesitating by the numerous messy, inky blots. When she finishes, she lays the pen on the counter and looks at my grandmother and me, and I shove my ink-stained hand deeper into my pocket. "Lots of changes," the clerk says, a statement I'm sure is directed at me.

I'm about to confess when my grandmother gets up on her toes to achieve another inch of height over the countertop. She fiddles with one of the buttons of her pink suit jacket. "Isn't that allowed?" she says in a voice that quavers, not intentionally.

The clerk hesitates: the British accent, the little spots of rouge, one now divided by a tear track, the thick eyeglasses and the pearl necklace with its heavy clasp pulling it down, the freckled bony chest and the ringed fingers all crooked with rheumatism. "No," the clerk says. "It's all right. You can change them."

"That's good," my grandmother says. "Sometimes my first answers are . . ." she pauses. "Impulsive," she says.

The woman nods, slowly. She hands my grandmother the scored test. "Pass," she says. "Twenty-nine out of thirty." She directs us to the next station, where my grandmother smiles—beams—for the camera.

"We're not going to tell your grandfather," she says, back in the car.

"Or Mom," I add.

"No one." She seizes my hand and holds it in her own, dry and hot as always. The need for secrecy, for further subterfuge, gilds what has been a wonderful experience—defying the machine of ordinariness, the terrifying bureaucracy that seeks to discount and deny her peculiar identity, refusing to admit what I have long ago understood: there is no one like my grandmother, a woman whose gifts cannot be measured by any reductive process intended for the masses and inherently insulting.

"You know how idiotic it was! You saw it," she says, as if reading my thoughts, and I nod. "How low-down and dishonest. They try to trick you, and it has nothing to do with driving! And you—everyone!—knows I can drive!"

I nod. She is, actually, an excellent driver.

"What would you like?" she says, eager to reward me, to adjust things between us so she's not in my debt. "Dinner out? A movie? New clothes?"

I don't answer.

"What?" she says again, maneuvering her big car into the congestion of Van Nuys Boulevard, heading toward home, her new temporary license in her bag. And she repeats the question when the mail brings the permanent one bearing her wide, laminated smile.

"I promised you a reward," she reminds me.

"No," I say.

The next time, in anticipation of her eighty-third birthday, we schedule our visit to the DMV into my spring break from college, and I come home with a day or two to spare—"to quiz me" as my grandmother cajoles over the phone—and we do pretend to study the manual together. At the dinner table, after my grandfather has retired to the den, we open the book and I ask her practice questions, some of which she answers correctly. But once inside the big beige building, sitting in the battered, dirty school desk, smaller and more wrinkled, if no less rouged, she doesn't even bother to fill in any answers.

"I thought it would be easier for you if I didn't make a mess of it," she whispers, loudly, as she passes the un-smudged test under the metal partition in the rest room.

Premeditation aggravates my nervousness, but she is calm in the stall next to mine. "The lady was very nice," she goes on. "She said it was fine for me to use the toilet. Maybe because I'm so old," she adds as an afterthought, and she laughs.

"Can't you be quiet!" I hiss. She stops talking, but drops her handbag and spills its contents, sniffing loud wet amplified sniffs, in case I don't know I've hurt her feelings. Her compact of rouge rolls like a wheel from under her stall door and comes to rest by a sink, where someone picks it up and says, loudly, "I've left it here, on the shelf under the mirror."

I flush my toilet, over and over, to drown out distractions, and, balanced on one side of the seat, finish taking the test. I shove it into the pocket of her handbag, open and waiting on the floor of her stall, and return to the waiting area, where I slouch behind a book and try not to watch her return to her desk in the test area. She sits for a few minutes, bent with unnatural attention over the page, adjusting my check marks, making my lines her own by drawing over them.

"What can I get you?" she asks in the car, on the way home. "What do you want, darling?"

I shake my head, and we drive in silence, both of us, perhaps, trying to make out the future that lies beyond the brown pall of Los Angeles smog. How many years before this won't work? Before she can't drive, and before the examiners are those that can't be tricked?

"You take the test, darling," she'll joke, a fiberoptic camera peering inside her while I hold her hand, hot and dry. "You pass it for me."

Seven. Seven years. But we don't know that yet. We can't guess. The green hills of Coldwater Canyon climb through the smog. Balanced on their slender posts, cantilevered houses hang over abrupt emptinesses. "They ought to fall down," she says, as she says each time we drive by them. She disapproves of such architecture. "No visible means of support," she adds, laughing as she always does when she says the phrase, finding it funny.

At home, she gets out of the car and steps carefully around a green puddle of coolant, leaked from my car, not hers. "Nothing?" she tries a last time.

"No," I say, and I give her a kiss.

But the next day, when I go back to school, she follows me to my car, parked in the driveway. It's early in the morning, my grandfather is still in bed, and she's in her dressing gown—*bathrobe* isn't a word she uses. She's carrying her handbag, and from it she pulls out an envelope and hands it through the open window. For a moment we're both holding it as we look at each other. "Drive safely," she says, crying as she does whenever I leave. "Call when you get in."

I wait until I'm at a gas station in Bakersfield to open the envelope. Ten twenty-dollar bills wrapped in a note: "One always wants something," it says, an impersonal—uncharacteristic—way for her to express herself.

Not her, not me. *One.*

WHAT REMAINS

A few years ago, Guernsey's, a New York City auction house, sponsored an event advertised as "the greatest rock and roll auction of all time." Among the four thousand items consigned for sale were electric guitars played by Jimi Hendrix and Paul McCartney; previously unseen photographs of Janis Joplin, Mick Jagger, and Patti Smith; rare acetate recordings by Elvis Presley and personal effects including clothing, jewelry, drawings, lyrics scrawled on notebook paper, even old bath towels. I am not a collector of rock memorabilia, but I attended the auction's preview in Manhattan's Puck Building because I wanted to look at three items mentioned on the local news the previous evening. As it turned out, the three things I wanted to see were the same requested over and over by successive TV crews that I watched enter the Puck Building's ballroom and consult the young woman with the clipboard who was handling public relations. She smiled extravagantly as she pointed out potential objects of interest, but the eyes of the reporters glanced off all but the three, as described by the auction catalogue: B34A, "Washbasin from the apartment of John Lennon, the Dakota (72nd and Central Park West), New York City"; E257E, "Elvis Presley owned and used rechargeable Remington Razor . . . in original box"; and G126A, the "left-handed sunburst Stratocaster . . . smashed on stage by [Kurt] Cobain" and bearing "remnants of blood from Cobain's fingers on the pickguard."

Waiting my turn behind the television crews, I watched as one and then another cameraman stepped up to the late Mr. Lennon's sink and, balancing unsteadily on a box or stool, contrived to point the lens of his video camera into the sink's drain. Then I got my chance to examine the sink; a Kohler wall-mount with two stainless-steel legs and shiny clean faucet and knobs, it was unremarkable.

But, wait, what was that? Between the hygienically smooth white porcelain and the polished stainless-steel collar that circled the orifice of the drain was a narrow but definite band of brown crud. This residue, dug out with a fingernail or pin, would not have filled a teaspoon. What of John Lennon might have been preserved in the crevice encircling his washbasin's drain? What fragment of hair or skin, what molecule of saliva, mucus, possibly even blood, vomit, or piss? Anyone considering the purchase was assured that the plumbing was accompanied by an "affidavit verifying the circumstances" from the "gentleman who did the repairs and retained the sink offered herein."

Perhaps whoever bought the sink, the opening bid for which was set at $6,000, has now collected and swallowed the dried sink scum, just as visitors to Goa, on the west coast of India, have bitten off two of the toes of Saint Francis Xavier, who died in 1552 and whose body, subsequently enshrined in the Portuguese colony, continues to draw crowds of pilgrims and miracle seekers. It is not an implausible idea. Who we consider holy changes over the centuries; what we want from them has not.

After her cremation, my own grandmother's ashes were returned to me by the Dunn Funeral Home in a white cardboard box bearing a yellow label whose return address was that of Brooklyn's Green-Wood Cemetery. Inside the white box was a thick black plastic one whose lid I pried at with a knife until it opened with a loud crack to reveal a polyurethane bag closed with a red twist tie, the kind that bakeries use. I took the bag out and held it in my lap. An average-sized human is said to yield seven pounds of cremated remains, about the weight of one of my grandmother's cats. The ashes felt as heavy as a cat, but were cool instead of warm. A certificate of cremation accompanying the bag bore this rubber-stamped message: VANDALISM FEE COLLECTED. This struck me as somewhat cryptic, but I guessed it was one of several supposed assurances that the ashes I held were indeed those of my grandmother, whose corpse was assigned a serial number by Green-Wood Cemetery, C 27594, which was inscribed on the boxes and all pertinent documents and stamped onto a coin I found among the ashes themselves when I opened the bag.

Ashes aren't so much ashes as fragments of burned bone, some large enough that I could observe the elegant tracery of the marrow's canals. These looked like lace, some white, others the color of rust; the rest was a fine gray dust that adhered to my fingers as I sifted through the remains. I withdrew my hand from the bag, sucked one finger, and felt the grit between my teeth. I licked the other fingers and my palm as well. Tasting what was left of my grandmother—a woman made holy to me by love and by blood—was something I did alone, behind the closed door to my study. The privacy of the act was not born of shame but of its being sacred: a last intimacy between two women who, in turn, had diapered each other. The following week, I poured the rest of her ashes into the sea; some were thrown back at me by the wind so that they stung my eyes and dusted my arms. I kept the bag within its two boxes and have occasionally pressed my face into it and inhaled.

What did I want from my grandmother's ashes? I have her temperament, I bear her features. Taking a little of her inside of me was not so much a superstitious reflex as it was a kind of communion: a private Eucharist.

The acquisition and veneration of relics reflect a primitive longing, one that has been carried forward from prehistory and has taken forms as various as cannibalism and Buddhism. Among cannibals, some are selective to the point that they eat a bit of brain for wisdom or heart for courage, supplements they hope will help them overcome their enemies in much the same way we expect iron tablets to defend us from anemia.

Even religions that are generally understood to eschew connection to the material world and to the body venerate the remains of the dead. In Yangon, Myanmar, construction of a great pagoda is under way. The building will enshrine one of the four teeth plucked from the Lord Buddha's cremation pyre in 483 B.C.E.; on some weekends thousands line up at the construction site to offer the gift of their labor. During the Middle Ages, Christian pilgrimages to shrines such as Spain's Santiago de Compostela (where, legend holds, the Apostle James was buried after Herod executed him in A.D. 42) were undertaken as journeys whose destinations were more spiritual than geographic. Such pilgrimages had their precedent in a long-standing classical tradition of travel to the site of important shrines, those housing either first-class, or corporeal, remains or what are called second-class, or representative, relics, personal items such as Achilles' spear, which is kept in the temple of Athena at Phaselis.

If we no longer expect the tomb of a hero to guarantee a town heavenly protection, it still offers economic solace. Graceland in Memphis, Tennessee, on whose grounds Elvis is buried, draws 700,000 tourists each year, 40,000 on the anniversary of his death. Cooperstown, New York, lures crowds to the National Baseball Hall of Fame and Museum, which enshrines Babe Ruth's glove, Ty Cobb's sliding pads, and the bat used by Mickey Mantle to hit a 565-foot home run. The New York Public Library owns pieces of Percy Shelley's skull. Yale's Beinecke Library includes a chamber pot used by FDR when he visited the university to receive an honorary degree. Americans who visit such reliquaries are doing what humans have always done: attempting to draw close to the sacred.

All of us persist against reason in believing that some manifestation of the dead's personality or spirit remains in his or her corpse, and our faith extends to include the dead's possessions, especially those objects that routinely come into direct contact with the body: clothing and tools used for eating or for grooming. At the auction preview, Elvis Presley's "Selektronic" razor, displayed in its original box lined with ersatz red velvet, and valued in the catalogue at $4,000, did indeed appear to have been used. The shaving head was dusted with what looked like skin and hair particles, and the corners of the box were gray with the same fine accumulation. Three days after I saw Presley's Remington, late-night talk-show host Conan O'Brien taped a segment at the auction and was quoted by *The New York Times* as having said, "Maybe I'll buy Elvis's electric shaver. I'll open it up and look for stubble and then auction it off, hair by hair." It was a joke, but a serious one. Just as the Catholic Church attempts to protect the corpses of saints from the kind of worshipful abuses visited on Francis Xavier's feet, displaying holy remains behind iron grilles or under glass, so Elvis's razor was locked in a case, the glass door of which was smeared with greasy handprints and fogged with breath; one cameraman wiped it off before he began videotaping.

A few miles uptown from the Puck Building, New York City's Mother Cabrini shrine houses what is described in one guidebook as the "mummy" of Saint Frances Xavier Cabrini, the first United States citizen to have been canonized. The shrine is in a chapel on the campus of Mother Cabrini High School. A religious gift shop serves as an antechamber and carries an assortment of pious trash familiar to those who frequent such concessions: tiny plastic squirt bottles filled with holy water, rosaries and laminated felt scapulars made in the Philippines, statuettes, pocket prayer books, votive candles. But the Cabrini gift shop also functions as a mini-museum, its walls lined with the kind of display cases that elsewhere in the high school might hold team trophies or biology specimens. Through their glass doors visitors can examine Frances Cabrini's personal articles, among them a tightly coiled gold spring, approximately two inches long. Presented with it is a Xerox copy of a handwritten letter that begins, "My father, Hugo Ragaini, felt gravely honored to have been fortunate enough to make dentures for Mother Cabrini. When she came to him in 1914 to have new dentures made, she told him to keep the gold spring which came from the original dentures she had made in France. . . ." (Before dentures were fixed in place by adhesive cream, springs were used to keep uppers from falling closed onto lowers.) The letter goes on to describe a miracle of healing attributed to Mother Cabrini's denture spring, which the signer, Victor Ragaini, hereby bequeaths to the saint's shrine as a token of his gratitude.

Cabrini's physical remains are laid in a glass coffin that forms the base for the main altar of her chapel. The top is marble, but you can see the saint through the coffin's sides. If you've watched the Disney version of *Snow White,* the casket looks very much like the one in which the dwarfs preserve their beloved housekeeper until her prince can come to wake her. This iconographic resemblance may be disturbing, but it is not accidental, for it is in anticipation of the Prince of Peace's resurrecting kiss that Frances Cabrini waits in preternatural sleep. The Church's use of symbols is determined by their potency, not their source, and many elements of fairy tales have been appropriated into hagiography. Saint Cabrini wears a gold crown; her face and hands project from a deflated, seemingly empty black habit. Below its hem, her shoes stick up and eerily recall another fantasy image. You suspect that were you to remove them, the saint's toes would shrivel, curl, and draw up under her habit.

Crouched by the casket on my hands and knees, I examined Mother Frances's hands and face. I wasn't prepared to accept her remains as being supernaturally incorrupt, but what I could see of her looked to be a remarkable embalming job. The side of the coffin was fogged with my nervous breath. Clearly, visitors were not expected to approach the saint so intimately, and, afraid of being found prostrated next to Frances with nothing but a pane of glass between us, I returned to the gift shop, presided over by a taciturn nun. "Is the body under the altar really Mother Cabrini?" I asked, beginning my question boldly but swallowing its last words. The nun made no response. She was one of those people who blink less frequently than the rest of us.

"What I mean to say is—" I paused. "Is what I see in the casket really Saint Cabrini?"

"Yes," said the nun. From behind the cash register, she crossed her arms over her habit.

"So the, uh, face and the hands, they aren't, uh—?" I was thinking wax, but the nun's impassive expression didn't allow me to utter the word.

"That's her," said the nun. I found it impossible to look her in the eye. My gaze ascended only as far as the obligatory spinster's mustache that softened the hard set of her lips. The phone in the gift shop rang, and when she turned to answer it I left. Later, I learned that the saint's remains, exhumed in 1933 for examination by a papal commission, had been placed within a wax effigy five years later.

In the early Church, the Eucharist was commonly celebrated over the remains of a saint. The cult of martyrs was dropped—not unlike Dorothy's Kansas farmhouse—right onto the Greek worship of heroes. The subjects of veneration were replaced, but the custom of honoring the dead persisted, with one difference. The Greeks, who did not believe in an afterlife (the shades in the underworld were just that: dim memories of the lives that preceded them), buried corpses intact and did not disturb their graves, whereas early Christians were soon tearing up knuckles and gristle and hair. The relics trade, which would be condemned by leaders of the Reformation, reached its peak in the Middle Ages, when relics served a number of important functions for the dissemination of Catholicism. For a faith that is founded upon the idea of resurrection of body as well as soul, the literal creation of altar from tomb is an important symbolic act, and Rome required the presence of a martyr's relic for the official consecration of an altar. The Holy Office tried to control the establishment of new churches by dictating what was and was not a martyr's bona fide remains, but, not surprisingly, relics proliferated as quickly as Elvis sightings.

Every sainted excrescence and fluid was discovered and produced. The Virgin's milk was stored in vials all over Christendom—so much of it that Calvin remarked wryly that even if Mary had been a cow, she could not have produced such a quantity in a mere lifetime. No one who could afford it was without some fleshly talisman, at the least a thread of someone's shroud or veil. For the common masses, the third-class, or substitute, relic was invented and persists today in such commercial pilgrimage centers as Lourdes. There, a bit of cloth that has supposedly touched a first- or second-class relic of Saint Bernadette is attached to an image of the saint and sold for an affordable price.

The contemplation of relics, Catholic or secular, has not encouraged my faith in resurrection any more than pressing the bag that once held my grandmother's ashes to my lips allows me to believe in her continued life. I am drawn to artifacts of the dead because through them I can approach death. Thus I was fascinated by a number of Frances Cabrini's garments hanging in the gift shop. Made of white linen or cotton, they were thin enough to appear as underclothes or nightgowns, and bore traces of the body that once filled them, including a mesmerizing, ghostly yellow stain in the lap of one. Did the saint spill her tea? Did she once lose control of some more intimate fluid? Whatever happened, the stain offered proof that a life passed through the fabric's embrace. The same proof rings the collars of shirts once worn by Elvis, stained their venerated armpits. Among Elvis's garments to be auctioned were a pristine white cardigan sweater (pressed flat under the glass of a frame) and a yellow silk shirt, shoulders drooping disconsolately off the hanger, cuffs in disrepair, stained at the neck. The dirty shirt was valued at $25,000 more than the clean sweater.

If we do not fancy ourselves as prone to superstition and magical thinking as medieval Christians, if we do not generally carry relics on our bodies in lockets and purses, in special rings, bracelets, and chokers, in order that they might deliver us from temptation and sin in this life and from hell in the next, still we fear what we have always feared—our own deaths. Afraid and therefore fascinated by the unthinkable end of ourselves, we need help in approaching a notion so alien and impossible that our society judges its clinical evidences obscene, something to be masked by the embalmer's art. For those of us who do not invest them with miraculous power, relics of the dead offer more pragmatic and humble gifts. They help us toward the challenging task of thinking about not being. And they comfort us through their mute witness, their not allowing mortality to mean erasure. The dead, they testify, *were*.

Is it because I have had more occasions to consider death than most women my age that I find the remains of the dead, both their bodies and their possessions, so compelling? My grandparents and my mother all died before I turned thirty, within the same few years. I saved relics of each of these people I loved: locks of hair, photographs, jewelry, letters. And, as if that were not enough mourning, in the time between and surrounding their deaths I visited other graves and other shrines. In Los Angeles, where I grew up, I saw DiMaggio's rose, replaced daily outside Marilyn Monroe's tomb. In the reliquary at Madrid's Monasterio de la Encarnación, I saw a tiny gold-stoppered bottle of the dried blood of Saint Pantaléon, which is said to be 1,600 years old and is believed to liquefy every twenty-seventh of July, on the saint's feast day.

It is blood that I've looked at with the greatest fascination: stains and smears and crumbs of a substance both humble and mysterious. In the wake of the chemotherapy that destroyed her marrow, my mother received a number of transfusions, and I watched their startling testimony to blood's life and power, saw their blush infuse her white cheeks. The reprieves were brief, only as long as blood lives: two months, no more, for whole blood includes newborn cells that may expect to live for up to 120 days as well as cells that die even as they enter the recipient's bloodstream.

Seduced long ago by Catholic iconography's eroticized images of stigmata, of martyrdoms, of Christ's opening his robes and his breast to reveal his bleeding heart, I cannot help but associate blood with expiation and with grief. After my grandmother's death, I compulsively donated my own blood every eight weeks, as often as the Red Cross would take it, in what I've only recently understood as my acting out a controlled mourning. At the donor center, a technician whom I too easily confused with an acolyte would relieve me of only so much of my grief: one pint. The act was my assertion that I would contrive to have grief stanched long before I died of it.

At the auction preview, I saved Kurt Cobain's blood-stained guitar for last and stood before it longest, while the white plate under the strings of the smashed Stratocaster shined silver under the portable klieg lights of successive TV crews. One of the guitar's metal strings, perhaps the one on which the dead singer had cut his fingers, was broken; it zigzagged crazily away from the tight rank of its neighbors, making, no doubt, a little silver shiver for the camera's eye to record. As advertised, the white pick guard did bear visible traces of blood. Without that stain, would the guitar have been valued at $15,000? Would someone have paid, as he or she did, $19,550?

Like the martyrs of the early Church, Kurt Cobain is famous for having died. His name was unknown to me before he killed himself. And though I could not name a single song or lyric by Kurt Cobain, I was moved by the sight of his blood spilled on his guitar. I found it impossible not to read it as a foreshadowing of his taking his own life. Because most of us fear suffering so intensely, we are awed by evidence of it. And in order to help us accept its inevitability, we invest pain with meaning; we revere sufferers and sentimentally imagine that misery is universally (rather than rarely) ennobling, that it sanctifies. For fifty cents you can purchase a prayer by Mother Cabrini inscribed on a laminated card: "The knowledge of suffering is the knowledge of the saints. He who does not know what Christian suffering is, what can he know of greatness and wonder in his days?" Do these words make an exclusively Catholic prayer? Can you not remove the word *Christian* and any limiting definition of the word *saint* and read it as a general human confession?

Abraham Lincoln was not a Catholic, but in American terms he is a saint. He has earned that status for his statesmanship, but no less for his suffering, which we believe we can see in his very face: lean, ascetic, as long and lugubrious as an El Greco. Man of sorrows, martyr, champion of the persecuted, Lincoln could not be anyone who enjoyed his life as much as well-heeled Jefferson or piggy-jowled Franklin. To be worthy of a reliquary, he would have to have been a man whose log-cabin birth was as humble as an arrival in a manger, whose childhood was doubly blighted by poverty and the death of his mother.

The National Museum of Health and Medicine, run by the Armed Forces Institute of Pathology and located on the grounds of the Walter Reed Army Medical Center in Washington, D.C., began its collecting activities during the Civil War. It greets visitors with a large, artfully lit glass case containing souvenirs of the autopsy performed on President Lincoln, as well as some from the autopsy of his assassin, John Wilkes Booth, including two bloodstained shirt cuffs once worn by army assistant surgeon Edward Curtis. In 1865, Curtis participated in Lincoln's autopsy, during which his shirt was splashed with the dead president's blood. There is an illicit quality to the relic, in part conferred by brown stains on yellowed cotton, which remind even the most reverent viewer of dirty underwear. But this humble aspect is part of what moves us, because we half expect that the blood of Lincoln would be different from our own, would have a luminosity, a molecular shiver. Because it is brown and dull and faded—utterly unremarkable—it witnesses to the grace of God or of fate, to whatever force can lift a poor boy from obscurity and make him our president.

I consider myself less a patriot than a Catholic, but the blood of Abraham Lincoln, along with the gray curls shorn from around his wound, brought unexpected tears to my eyes. Why? In part because I consider locks of hair as baby's mementos, all of which have an inherent melancholy: the reminder that time passes, that all babies age and die. But Lincoln's hair was forced right up against evil and violence, and it is the knowledge of what was bought with those curls that strikes us so viscerally. In Lisieux, France, there is a shrine to Saint Thérèse that includes her hair in a resplendent gold frame. The luxury of those long lustrous curls, shorn when she entered the Carmelite order at fifteen and saved by her sisters, together with an understanding of what austerity and suffering they bought, cannot fail to move visitors. Just as pilgrims to Lisieux are likely to believe that Thérèse's renunciation of the earthly pleasures symbolized by her frankly sexual tresses paid her way through gates of unimaginable splendor, so does the pilgrim to the Lincoln shrine accept his grizzled curls, lost in the wake of an assassin's bullet, as part of the price of admission to a different pantheon. Perhaps this is why Indiana University's Lilly Library bought Sylvia Plath's childhood curls in 1978, fifteen years after her suicide;

their arrested innocence is made all the more powerful by what would follow in the poet's life—and vice versa.

The Lincoln exhibit includes one of several probes used to locate the bullet in Lincoln's brain, skull fragments removed from the wound, and the bullet itself, all of which keep close company with sections of spinal cord and vertebrae from John Wilkes Booth. I find the choice to enshrine the assassin's relics with those of the martyr surprising, and even a casual visitor is disturbed by this conjugal juxtaposition of sacred and profane. I watched several people pass by the lit case. "I don't like that," said one old woman in a wheelchair, pushed by her grandson. "Don't like what?" he asked. "Sticking his things in with the others," she said, pointing at Booth's vertebrae.

Had the nuns who arranged Mother Cabrini's relics been given curatorial privilege over the Lincoln artifacts, they would have created a more agreeable display. Their sophistication, probably intuitive—nothing that could have been stipulated in a manual—was such that they divided the woman into her divine and earthly tendencies. Her belt of nails and the knotted scourge are in a separate cabinet from her silver hairbrush and buttonhook. All are sensual artifacts, but tools for grooming the soul are different from those intended for the pleasure of the body.

Gowns and hair and hairbrushes. Shavers, guitars, washbasins. Things that once belonged to people we did not ever touch or speak with, people whose fame allows them the immortality of their stories but cannot halt the decay of their bodies or the inevitable denouements of their private, real lives. If Abraham Lincoln, Elvis, Babe Ruth, and all the saints are not endowed with powers enabling them to escape death, then who is? In the *Iliad*, Homer tells us that Achilles was given the choice of a short heroic life or a long unre-markable one. He chose to die a hero. Later, when Odysseus encounters him in the *Odyssey*, Achilles' shade bitterly laments such folly. Poetic license allows the dead Achilles to know what he could not and we cannot yet fully understand: life ends.

My grandfather was the first member of my immediate family to die. I was twenty-three. He took long enough to die that, as I anticipated my loss, I had time to break down my fear into its parts. I was afraid of the pain I would feel at losing the companionship and protection of the man who was for me a father. But I was also afraid of death—not my grandfather's particular death but the unapproachable and unavoidable fact of human mortality. What if my grandfather should die in my presence? I worried that I might have to witness his turning from living to dead flesh. I had never before seen a corpse.

A cool, previously hidden pragmatism led me to prepare myself. I looked up funeral notices in the *Los Angeles Times,* picked out the nearest mortuary that advertised a "viewing" of a man of advanced years, and went to look at the em-balmed corpse of someone I didn't know. I had the good for-tune of an uninterrupted visit—there were no legitimate mourners to see as I leaned into the casket and brushed the corpse's cheek, touched its immobile, cool lips. How straightforward death was! I nearly laughed in relief. A month later, when I kissed my grandfather good-bye, I hugged his body in unabashed affection. Here was what had supported, given form and substance, to the person I had loved all my life. I brought scissors to the hospital morgue and cut a curl, which I still have, as well as his glasses and cardigan sweater, a pair of wooden shoe trees.

Among what I have of my dead mother are two of her baby teeth, saved by my grandmother in a tiny glass-

stoppered vial of rubbing alcohol. The teeth, in the senti-
mental vernacular of baby mementos, recall pearls, but in
each a brown root cavity bears traces of her blood. They are
a double relic because, beyond my mother, they attest to her
own mother's love, which counted them of value, saved and
bottled them. And they exist within generations of my family's baby teeth, generations that include my own and my
daughter's. Holding the little bottle, I can't not consider my
children and what, after I am dead, they might keep of me
and hold in their hands.

Sitting in a doctor's office, I ask a question that occurred
to me as I was looking through my desk drawer for some
Post-Its. "I have samples of my mother's hair," I tell him,
"and my grandmother's, and her mother's, as well," leaving
out the confession that I keep such mementos—along with
my husband's extracted wisdom teeth, various hospital
bracelets, an anonymous finger bone from a Mexican cemetery—in among my stationery supplies. "Should I submit
them for genetic testing for BRC1 or 2?"

The doctor, a kind man in his sixties who delivered all my
babies, held their new, blood-bathed life in his hands, doesn't
answer. Instead he writes a phone number on a pad of paper.
He tears the sheet off and hands it to me. "You'll have to talk
to a genetic counselor," he says. "I can't advise you on this."

The relics of the dead, my dead, may trace a gene for
breast cancer through generations, back to my great-
grandmother, who, like my mother, died of it. I keep the
number—keep the folded paper in the drawer that holds the
locks of hair, staples, wisdom teeth—but I never call for an
appointment.

In the last months of my grandmother's life, she wore a mo-
hair scarf wrapped around her waist, hidden under the blan-

kets of her bed. She was not cold but afraid. Without this security object she could not rest, and she allowed no one to take it from her, not even long enough to launder it. In the end, it was bloodstained from a wound I caused while bathing her one morning. She had sat hunched over for so long that a fold of skin at her waist grew together, and when I washed it I tore the adhesion open; it began to bleed and never healed. After my grandmother died, I didn't consider laundering the scarf any more than whoever bought Elvis's dirty shirt did, or the curator who guards the stained cuffs of Lincoln's autopsy surgeon. Clean, it would tell me nothing.

When I hold the scarf, I hold both my grandmother's and my own death in my hands. The scarf and I inform each other. Only I can tell the story it bears; only such an object can tell me what my helpless trips to the donor center belied: one day blood, and grief, will flow unchecked.

NITPICKERS

Late on the Saturday afternoon following Thanksgiving, I'm standing in the supermarket checkout line with my nine-year-old daughter. Cereal, juice, milk, pasta. Bananas, yogurt, cookies. My daughter's pullover is dirty, her long brown hair tangled, only half of it left in the ponytail holder. I watch her scratch her head.

"Stop it," I say.

"I can't."

"But you know how itching is. Scratching makes it worse."

She sighs. "Can I have a quarter?" she asks.

"If I have one." My pockets are filled with receipts, dirty tissues, an apple core, sandwich rinds, and even Milk-Bone crumbs, detritus from the day spent on the road, all of us—two parents, two children, the dog—returning from a holiday spent at Colin's parents'.

My daughter turns the handle of the vending machine and retrieves the gum ball with her left hand, continuing to scratch with her right. Children do scratch, of course, and they slouch; they sneeze and yawn without covering their mouths; they worry their loose teeth with dirty fingers. I make it a point to resist unnecessary censure, but this scratching—dedicated, passionate—for some reason it bothers me. Suddenly I remember a letter from the school nurse two weeks prior, the one that informed parents of fourth graders of a case of head lice in their child's class. I stare as my daughter's ponytail holder slides off and onto the floor, dislodged by the force of her scratching.

"Didn't go through," the checkout girl says. "Maybe you should watch while you punch in your PIN number," she suggests, sarcasm sharpening her tone.

I run my debit card back through the slot. *Not head lice, please not head lice,* I pray, and yet I know it must be lice that's causing the itching. For wouldn't their arrival be that of a long-expected blight? The consummation of a dread fueled by conversations with other mothers, anecdotes traded over the phone as we preside over our respective kitchens, overlooking homework and saucepans, pencil in one hand, slotted spoon in the other. We navigate the small panic of the working mothers' dinner hour with telephone receivers cradled between ear and shoulder, glasses of wine we'd rather share in person, but where would we find the time? It was just the previous month that I adjusted the receiver to whisper, *You forgot to carry over into the tens,* a drip of olive oil staining my daughter's homework, then asked, "But what happened, really? Not an actual breakdown."

"Well, you know, she ended up having her daughter's head shaved."

"Not *shaved.*"

"Okay, a crew cut. And she broke up with the guy she was seeing. And she went back into therapy."

"Yeah," I'd conceded. Head lice could do that.

I hurry my daughter out of the market, hustle her across streets, hissing, as though a passerby might care to eavesdrop, "I think you might have lice."

She stops scratching. "Really?" she says, and she pauses midstep, looking more interested than alarmed.

I pull her along the sidewalk, hand tight around her biceps, remembering how I resented that same businesslike grasp and yet unable, under the circumstances, to be gentle. "I have to look," I pant. "With a good light. A magnifying glass."

At home, I sit my daughter under a halogen reading lamp. I can't find the magnifier, but under the bulb's glare I don't need one to see that, yes, a tiny something is crawling on my daughter's scalp. Against her dark brown hair the louse looks slyly translucent, its minute gray legs moving with fugitive industry through her hair. I drop the hank I've separated, left with an impression not unlike a *National Geographic* cutaway of life in the grasslands—a menacing, miniature forest blown up for the purpose of edification, of exposing the clandestine life at root level. I smile at my daughter, I give her a hug and try not to do what I want to do, which is scream, weep, run. After all, I don't want her to feel unclean or stigmatized.

My husband, however, is not so often spared the fallout of my neuroses. "Something's happened!" I tell Colin, interrupting as he triages the mail that arrived during our absence. He doesn't answer, and I step dramatically between him and the pile of bills on his desk. "Lice!" I announce.

Colin looks up. "Oh," he says, and then he pushes the phone bill toward me. "What are these 956 numbers? Is someone calling for horoscopes or something?"

"Head lice! Lice! Lice all over her head!" My husband looks at me. In fact, I've only seen the one louse, but its image—so fleeting, so furtive—has seized hold of my imagination in a way that a more explicit encounter might not have. Already one has multiplied into legions of vermin.

"What does that mean?" Colin asks carefully, his eyes straying back to the bill.

"It means that—that I have to go to the pharmacy, right now, before it closes! That we all have to wash our hair with lice killers. That I have to do the sheets and the towels and—"

"You want me to go to the pharmacy?" he offers, less out of generosity, I suspect, than out of a desire to avoid the first maneuvers in a campaign of bed stripping and late-into-the-night laundry. By virtue of the mothers' dinner hour network of rumor and information, I know what's required to rid a household of head lice: stuffed animals must be confiscated and sealed in plastic bags; clothing and all personal effects subjected to hours in a hot dryer; heads bowed under chemical rinses; hair raked with a nit comb until tears flow.

I look at Colin, who, like most husbands, lacks the ability to come back from the store with the right brand of detergent, the unbruised apple, the size of diaper that corresponds to the size of the person to be diapered. "I'll go," I say. "You'll get the wrong stuff."

"There's nothing I can do?" he asks, hopefully.

"You can put them in the bath. Start with her, and make sure her clothes go into a garbage bag, not the hamper. I'll be back in ten minutes."

Galvanized out of my post-holiday-six-months-pregnant-and-spent-the-day-on-the-turnpike torpor, I slam out of the house and arrive breathless and prickling with anxiety at the pharmacy, where I spend more than fifty dollars on one of each pediculicide the store carries. I hunch over the counter as I sign the credit card receipt, sure that all the people in line behind me with their suddenly not-so-embarrassing armloads of douches and ear wax dissolvers and hemorrhoid creams are watching me with disgust, stepping back to avoid even tangential contact with a person who is buying *the family-size pack of Nix lice-killing shampoo.*

A tear, one I recognize as worthy of a schoolchild, slides down my nose. My fifth-grade homeroom teacher, Mrs. Knowles, was tall and thin, with meticulously combed silver hair. Perhaps teaching was more vocation than economic necessity, because when the Southern California temperature dipped into the low fifties she wore a very un-schoolteacher-like black mink jacket that set off her hair in a manner that even children could appreciate. A fastidious person whose long, manicured fingers remained magically untouched by chalk dust or red ink, Mrs. Knowles was given to spontaneous lectures on personal hygiene. Routinely, she sent boys to the principal's office for the commonplace vulgarities of belching or nose picking. Girls were warned of the dangers of sharing hairbrushes, combs, scarves.

Head lice, she announced, were a *deserved affliction* that visited the slovenly; and when her black eyes rested briefly on my own head I knew that I must be infested. Clumsy, with unkempt nails, tousled hair, wrinkled blouse: I was a person whom lice would savor, and for weeks after school I sat on the tiled bathroom counter with a magnifying glass in one hand, a flashlight in the other, determined to catch one. That I never saw any evidence of lice did not convince me I wasn't a host, and I spent the remainder of fifth grade unable to meet Mrs. Knowles's penetrating gaze. As I was ashamed to raise my hand to produce answers I knew but was unworthy to utter, my grades fell. Surreptitiously, I spent my allowance and birthday money on medicated dandruff shampoo, thinking it might effect a cure. Behind the locked bathroom door I applied it full strength and left it on until my scalp tingled.

When I come home from the pharmacy, Colin is eating a peanut butter and jelly sandwich, his plate balanced on the bills.

"You were supposed to be putting her in the bath!" I cry.

He smiles. "I thought if I got myself something to eat you wouldn't have to worry about my dinner," he counters, still seeming calm, clearly unable to understand that we're embarking on a dire war.

The first night of the first campaign against lice is not, in retrospect, so bad. There are tears, yes. And, yes, the shampoo smells and burns, the combing hurts (nits, or louse eggs, are cemented to hair shafts with a seemingly bionic adhesive), and yes, the favorite stuffed toys are smothered in bags. But when at last we are all in bed, scrubbed and smarting, sister, brother, father, and even pregnant mother who failed to see any fine print cautioning people in her condition to avoid contact with pediculicides, I feel briefly optimistic. I've worked hard for hours. I'm going to win.

On Monday morning, I send a note to the school nurse, admitting, like a good citizen, that my daughter has had lice and that she and her brother were treated. My communication has a shrill quality and makes it clear that I hold the school responsible for our suffering. When I call the nurse later that day I try to sound friendly, but a querulous tone takes over.

The nurse sighs. She is patient. "People always hold the school responsible," she concedes, and then she tells me about a child whose persistent case of head lice was finally cured when the vector was identified not as a classmate but as the child's grandmother. The nurse offers to send a packet of information home with my daughter: alternative treatments, protocols of hygiene taken from *The Lice-Buster Book*, a pamphlet from a professional nit-picking service that will, if needed, come to one's house to end an infestation. I hang up feeling both rebuked and a little self-righteous.

Haven't I devoted days to this already? How can she imply that the scourge is not yet over?

By the time I get the packet, another week has passed, during which I have continued to launder and scrub and—uselessly, according to the Xeroxes—send out carpets to be steam cleaned. Alone in the house, aided by the unnatural strength granted by adrenaline, and ignoring the wisdom that dictates against pregnant women lifting heavy objects, I've heaved up beds, desks, and filled bookcases to pull out rugs which I've then rolled and carried down flights of stairs.

For two weeks we live on chilly floorboards, and then, just hours after the carpets have been returned—sanitized, deodorized, pet-guarded: I say yes to every potentially louse-unfriendly option—my son starts to scratch his head.

"It is true, is it not, that this isn't a medical emergency?" Over the breakfast dishes, my husband tries, quixotically, to combat hysteria with reason. "That lice can't really hurt the children?"

I nod, lick tears from over my lip. Exhausted after another night of chemical shampoos and 300-watt nit combing, I've slept only a few hours, tormented by nightmares of every imaginable dermatological blight, from baldness to leprosy.

"Lice don't carry diseases?" Colin presses.

I shake my head.

"So it's only pneumonia that might kill them?" He tries, uselessly, to get me to laugh. Subfreezing weather has arrived, and yet there's never a hat or a scarf to be found, all of them being gradually, day by day, reduced to dryer fluff.

What will end this scourge? According to the pamphlet from the lice-eradicating service, in the last several years a subgroup of the vermin has developed resistance to killing agents like Nix, a fact of which I am well aware, having watched lice swim with energetic defiance through tides of supposedly poisonous shampoos and creme rinses. And the products don't even claim to kill nits, an adult female laying as many as ten a day for thirty days . . . *each louse with three hundred potential children and*—I do the simple math over and over, the product seems impossible—*ninety thousand grandchildren* . . .

"There's this service," I offer. "They'll come to the house and—"

"How much does it cost?" Colin stands from the table.

"Sixty dollars."

He looks at me with suspicion. "Only sixty?"

"An hour," I add, apologetic.

"That's outrageous." Colin shakes his head, gathering papers into his briefcase. And he doesn't even know how much it cost to send the rugs out to be boiled.

I follow my husband through the front door, deafening myself to complaints about his missing hat, all his missing hats, and thinking dark thoughts about his handsome beard, his general hairiness, his affection for knit watch caps. It's probably him, *the vector,* why not? He claimed to have left the Nix on for fifteen minutes, but did he? He never reads package directions, considers weekends an excuse to forgo bathing, doesn't floss. Lies to his dentist about not flossing. At night I listen for sounds of him scratching; I make sure there's a wide moat between his pillow and mine.

On the street we head in opposite directions. Today I'm one of the parents who will accompany my daughter's class to a children's theater production of C. S. Lewis's *The Lion, the Witch, and the Wardrobe,* adapted from one of my favorite novels. Still, sitting among rows of elementary school students, all fidgeting, stretching, and scratching in their familiar and probably benign way, I can't watch the play, surrounded, as I feel I am, by happily squirming vermin carriers.

For Christmas we return to Colin's parents, this time to their Virginia cabin, driving through the pretty Blue Ridge mountains in our minivan, the vehicle that my father-in-law politely suggested might have been the original, Pandoral source of our infestation. Strewn with fast-food bags, dog hair, candy wrappers, smelling of fertilizer, mildew, indelible-even-if-long-past episodes of motion sickness, ours is a car that would fall under suspicion whenever health or hygiene was the issue.

But no, Colin tells his father, the car spends days locked up and unoccupied, and head lice are obligatory parasites, they need fresh blood every twelve hours.

This Christmas is, in most respects, one of the best we've had. The children are transported by their first skiing lessons, and Santa has been astonishingly extravagant: two new iMacs, purple for him, blue for her. Sitting among torn wrapping paper, my seams splitting with the promise of new life, my face shining in the festive glow of the tree, I feel cold with dread. Both sister and brother are scratching their heads, and what if the itch isn't dry skin brought on by so many caustic shampooings? Having reached the point where the children duck and run from examination and, worried as I am that they might give lice to their cousins, having been asked by Colin's mother not to reveal our unsavory blight, what can I do?

Toast crumbs. Pollen. Salt spilled from a shaker. Sawdust. Stray bits from a chemistry set: for me, every surface of the cabin crawls with lice. To keep anxiety at bay, I police the headgear situation, forbidding anyone to share hats, and each night sizzle everything in the dryer. In bed, under an immaculate winter sky, stars glittering in fiery immunity to human torment, I'm host to a wild nervous itching that targets my pubic region. Though I well know that head lice and pubic lice are not the same creature, it seems in the dark that these lice, *our lice,* might lack discrimination, and I succumb to the indignity of midnight searches, using a hand mirror and flashlight to see what my pregnant belly obscures from direct observation.

By the time we return home, I'm not only fretful but pessimistic. Still, I surprise myself with the storm of desperate tears occasioned by the third discovery of head lice, these, on both son and daughter, seeming to saunter insolently down the pathway made by the comb.

"I'm calling them," I say, and Colin doesn't need to ask who. I advance on him with comb in hand. "I'm not kidding. I can't take any more."

My husband's eyes crinkle in conjugal been-there-don't-go-there apprehension. "Call," he agrees, and then he says the one thing that tells me how desperate I must seem: "I don't care how much it costs."

It's 8:30 on a Wednesday morning when I dial the lice service and get a recorded message from a doctor, whose voice asks my name and number, in return offering a cell phone number in case of emergency. I write this down and consider dialing it—certainly, the presence of parasites on my children is a crisis. But is it an emergency? I can't imagine the conversation the faceless doctor and I might have, were he to answer. Would it begin with my predawn nightmare? *Together my children and I are falling down a long chute, like a laundry chute, at the bottom of which is a vat of something that's*

supposed to cure lice, except it doesn't, instead . . . It seemed un-
likely that a reliable professional would invite the kind of
hysteria overwrought mothers are capable of delivering.

I manage to wait until nine, when the doctor's assistant
returns my message. "Can you send someone today?" I
plead.

"I'll try. But I have to tell you," she cautions, "it's our busy
season." I hang up, reduced, until ten, to those petitionary
prayers it's embarrassing to make, even silently, to oneself.
Then the phone rings.

"Twelve-thirty," the assistant says.

"Do you take checks, credit cards? Should I get cash from
the bank?" I picture myself with a suitcase crammed with a
cartoon ransom of banded bills. Any amount to return my
children to me unharmed and deloused.

"Checks are fine." She warns me that it might require
many hours to one-by-one hand remove the nits from both
my children's heads—the only true method for eradicating
lice—and that the sixty-dollar-per-hour fee will not include
the cost of shampoos, oils, travel expenses, tips.

"Of course," I say, the banded bills shifting from twenties
to fifties. "I understand."

The doorbell rings at the appointed hour, and yet, when I
see two soberly dressed women on my front step, one carrying a dark folder and what appears to be a briefcase, their
missionary aspect and expressions of dire intervention de-
ceive me. They must be Jehovah's Witnesses, who frequently
proselytize in my neighborhood. I open the door, and they
both nod in a curt, businesslike way and step inside, out of
the cold, before I can politely refuse any tracts.

"Do you have a table where I can set up?" the one with
the briefcase asks.

"Oh." I look from one face to the other, confused. "You're from—you're the lice people?"

The woman who inquired about the table smiles with faint condescension. "You are Mrs. Harrison?" she counters.

In reply I step back and out of their way, inviting them farther into the hall. "The kitchen?" I suggest. Another curt nod, and the two follow me and watch as I peel back the holly print tablecloth to expose an edge to which they can clamp the base of a folding lamp produced from the black bag.

"Christmas," I offer in unnecessary explanation for the gaudy cloth, an old favorite of my grandmother's.

"Plug?" the woman asks, shedding her overcoat and gloves. The other continues to silently unpack equipment.

Apparently we are under way, having forgone any pleasantries of introduction. I call the children from their rooms and they creep reluctantly downstairs, for once stepping carefully on the creaking old treads.

The lamp is the kind I associate with the watchmaker's trade, a circular fluorescent bulb mounted around a large magnifying lens. Switched on, the bright eye illuminates a Mary Poppins–like production of items from the one deceptively small bag case: several gallon-capacity Ziploc bags, each holding four plastic applicator-tip bottles of amber liquids; a selection of fine-toothed combs and slender wooden sticks; a dozen large plastic hair clips, a bottle of rubbing alcohol and a shallow bowl in which to pour it; a roll of white paper towels; and a large, felt-backed, plastic tablecloth to unfold and spread on the floor.

Setup is efficient, accomplished without conversation. I and my two children watch in uncharacteristic silence, nodding submissively as the taller woman, who never offers her name and whose terse manner inhibits my asking it, explains that she will be doing today's job, her companion is here only as an apprentice, to observe. She hands me a form, one that includes questions about possible allergies, and as I complete it I understand that the emergencies to which the doctor's message alluded must be those of anaphylactic shock, some dangerously dire reaction to his formulas. I hesitate, briefly, before signing.

The first order of business is to check all our heads. My daughter sits in a chair placed under the circular bulb, and the nitpicker begins to examine her scalp, using one of the wooden sticks to part her thick hair. For the purpose of inspection she has donned intimidating headgear: glasses like those for welders, the heavy, square magnifying lenses set in a visor so cumbersome it requires additional bracing in the form of a band that goes over the top of her meticulously cornrowed hair. "See how I open the head," she says to her apprentice, and I shudder, helplessly, her words evoking playground accidents, split skulls. A few minutes later, after my son has had his turn and I am sitting with the light pouring over my shoulders, she repeats the phrase, and I hear "open" as though it pertained to a text, the content of my head easily readable under so many watts and powers of magnification.

When I stand up from the examination chair, the expensive nitpicker looks pointedly at my swollen midriff and asks, "Did you tell the office about this?" Having reached that point in pregnancy where people often address remarks to my middle rather than to my face, I'm used to people asking if I'm well while inquiring, really, about the progress of gestation; but how we're doing isn't what the nitpicker wants to know.

"Did I tell them I was pregnant?" I ask, feeling myself blush under her fixed stare, apologetic as an unwed teen.

She nods, lips pursed, conveying exasperation. With no evidence of lice and only one nit—"loose on the shaft," as the nitpicker describes it—I present a complication: I cannot be treated with the same shampoo as that indicated for use on my children.

I shake my head. "I didn't think—" *I had any,* I was going to add.

"Where's the phone? I have to call."

I show her to the desk. "Is it necessary?" I ask. "For just one? If it was loose, not really stuck to the hair . . . Maybe it was dead?" I suggest, hopefully. What I don't dare articulate is my suspicion that she was mistaken, maybe it wasn't even a nit, or perhaps the nit is made up, a ruse to extort even more money from her captive client—for how can a person have a single egg, and that in the absence of its parent? How likely is it that a solitary unwed louse would have so quickly traversed the forest of my hair, leaving one lone offspring in her wake? But the nitpicker, already in consultation with the office that dispatched her, doesn't answer my questions.

Standing over my daughter, working up a pungent lather, the nitpicker conveys the tenacious, the steadfast if weary, quality of our own convent-trained Belizean nanny. The doctor who owns this service must be quite rich—as prosperous as the agent through whom we found our nanny— having intelligently capitalized on the squeamishness of women like me: mothers who have tried and failed, who have enough money and not enough patience to forgo the expertise of one of his employees, women perhaps all like the one standing in my kitchen, smoothly dark and industrious, with a melodious island accent, a disdainful mien, and a youth that prepared her for the possibility of relentlessly tedious tasks. Our nanny has worked for us for ten years now, wiping up spills and tears, arranging play dates and walking the blocks between them, flinching at the casual profanities

that sometimes issue from the largely secular mass of pre-
dominantly white and affluent children in whose company
she finds herself. Our nanny, I know, loves and disapproves
of us in equal measure. The nitpicker only disapproves.

"Do I have to be treated?" I ask her. It's now a half hour
after she has hung up with her office, time during which I've
waited for her to reveal whatever verdict proceeded from the
exchange, monosyllabic on our end.

"Ask the doctor. Only he know," she says. This is, I discover, a standard response. Though I never meet or speak
with the calm voice that has masterminded this war against
lice, it is his hidden wisdom that will dictate the precaution
of treating my head's micro-infestation with a special solution formulated for pregnant and nursing mothers (and delivered, hours after a second phone consultation, to my
door), his wisdom that mandates the follow-up applications
of shampoos and oils and vermin-repellent drops.

"What's in it?" I ask of the golden, thick-as-honey liquid
the nitpicker has worked into my daughter's hair.

She takes her time answering questions. "Ask the doctor," she says, finally, when she leads my daughter to the
sink.

As for my repeated question of the significance of the nit
being "loose" on my hair shaft, she tells me that she believes
this to mean the egg is "no good" but concedes that this may
be one of the many "mits about nits," her accent biting the
end of the word *myth* down to a hard *T*.

With a wooden skewer about half the length of those
used for shish kebab, the nitpicker parts my daughter's hair
into sections, clipping back all but one at the nape of the
neck. Then, again with the skewer, she separates perhaps ten
or twenty hairs from the section and scrutinizes them under
the lamp and through the headgear.

Although I can't read the expression in the nitpicker's

eyes, every so often I catch a glimpse of one, huge and Cyclo-
pean, behind the magnifying lens. Spiked with lashes of
Betty Boop–like proportion, it reveals a margin of white
sclera all the way around the iris and gives her an aspect of
preternatural sensitivity that I associate with certain photographs of Marcel Proust, reports of his rooms baffled with
cork to protect their famously neurasthenic inhabitant.
Below the visor, the disdainful nostrils, I watch the nitpicker's mouth, learning to read the small movements that
accompany her task. When she finds nothing, her pretty lips
are closed and immobile, but upon the discovery of a nit, she
purses them a little more tightly and maintains their rigor as
she grasps the egg with her fingers and slides it down the ten
or twelve inches of the hair shaft. Holding the tiny thing
tightly between index finger and thumb, she rinses it from
their tips in the waiting bowl of alcohol and wipes them on a
paper towel. Then, having made this much progress, she re-
laxes her mouth into its former, not quite so stern attitude,
and moves on to the next afflicted hair.

The process by which each nit is detected, grasped, and
eradicated has the smooth elegance of any set of motions that
has been practiced countless times, motions, like those of
spinning, for example, that a novice performs with seemingly palsied clumsiness. The methodical concentration I
witness teaches me how laughably inadequate my efforts
have been. Of course I knew, somewhere I knew, that I
wasn't getting all the eggs by combing, but how quickly I
succumbed to the pressure of tears. How quickly, in retrospect, I gave up. I find myself fantasizing about turning any
number of ill-completed tasks over to a professional. What if
someone like this paragon of quiet industry were to apply a
comparable thoroughness to alphabetizing our library,
cleaning out closets, updating the address file?

As she works, the nitpicker murmurs homilies to her apprentice about patience, diligence, the value of a job well done, and in each instance I find myself lacking. This is the kind of work that progress has not altered, an unpleasant task to which I applied the wishful new-world alchemy of science, money, and convenience: a box from the drugstore costing $22.99 and containing two bottles of Nix, a plastic comb, a printed page of instructions, and, of course, an 800 number. What is required is old-world tenacity, hands that glean the grain, card the wool, weed the acres.

Under such hands, my daughter behaves with exemplary self-control. Not yet ten years old, she is no more patient nor docile than anyone would expect of a child her age. But on this afternoon she will sit, still and quiet, for more than five hours of hair pulling, a book in her lap, eyes trained on its pages, sometimes overbright with tears but never once flashing with the wild anger occasioned by my own attempts at this chore. Unexpectedly, there is a peace to this wan winter tableau—a calm both demanded of us by the nitpicker and proceeding from our humble recognition that a stubborn problem is being eradicated through sheer perseverance.

I sit, my own work before me, in an effort at redemption. If I cannot myself delouse my child, at least I can keep her company while the job is done, I can apply myself to earning the money that I'll hand over to the lice removal agency— more than five hundred dollars for the seven hours the nitpicker will spend in my home. But the women's raptness, as if they were engrossed in a fascinating rather than monotonous occupation, distracts me. Again and again I find my eyes straying from my own work back to the three faces held in the halo of light.

My daughter bears a pout reminiscent of her toddler years. Her cheeks are flushed, a dark lock hides her forehead, and she's cracked the spine of her book, opening it wide to see a photograph more clearly. It's *The Guinness* (*Guy-ness,* as she calls it) *Book of World Records,* a cheap paperback version bought in an airport to while away a layover, and strikes me as almost the obligatory companion for this trial. Even its title is one I associate with tedium, with sifting through the relentlessness of human experience, searching for the amusing exception. This edition (its twenty-fourth, published in 1988) contains the same photographs that fascinated me as a child: Ethel Granger's grotesque thirteen-inch waist; Shridhar Chillal's curling fingernails, totaling 158 inches in length and painted in stripes of alternating colors; the morbidly obese motorcycle-riding twins. The illustrations, small and underexposed, render their subjects all the more mysterious, unknowable, and I watch as my daughter scrutinizes each. Freaks are few, and most of life consists—like nitpicking—of unrelieved repetition. Head lice are a commonplace affliction, unlike that of Charles Osborne of Anthon, Iowa, who hiccuped for sixty-five years straight.

The nitpicker stands from her chair, perhaps to relieve her back more than to get a better perspective on my daughter's head, and exhales a long, tension-filled sigh. Two hours have passed, a long time to examine not even one half of one head, and a very long time for a child to sit with forbearance while a stranger pulls her hair. I catch my daughter's eye, and at my expression of sympathy her chin wobbles, she picks the book up from her lap and shields her face from compassion: too proud to cry in front of these women she does not know.

"Maybe a little break?" I suggest, timidly. "A glass of orange juice? A chance to go to her room for a new book?"

The nitpicker nods, a brief dip of her head that conveys less acquiescence than indulgence. She is made of tougher stuff than we, it says.

In the bathroom, my daughter and I hug, and she deliberately smears my bulging middle with tears and mucus. "It's boring!" she says. "It hurts!" She stamps her feet. "This is ruining a whole day! A whole day will be gone!"

"I know, I know," I say, and I placate, I bribe. Why is it that, like an old woman, my daughter counts her days and even her hours? Is she already the child of her parents, always conscious of mortality, begrudging each misspent minute?

"As soon as it's over," I promise, "we'll go to J&R Computer World." We'll look for a game to play on her new iMac. "Maybe the one where you can build a better Rome, or—"

"I want the whole store!" she says, a measure not of greed but of torment. "That's what it will take to make up for this!" She forgets to cry quietly, forgets the women on the other side of the bathroom door, and I'm reassured by her anger, relieved to see that the unnervingly stoic child I've been watching is, after all, my little girl, capable of great self-control, and of temper tantrums. "Why did this have to happen?" she wails. "Why did it happen to me?"

I give my standard response to tribulation, which always recalls a snippet of Indian television I saw more than eleven years ago, in a hotel in New Delhi. Tired, dirty, jet-lagged, my husband and I sat dully before an old black-and-white set that offered one channel, one program. A dusky talk-show host, looking like a subcontinent David Letterman, interviewed a turbaned ascetic who sat cross-legged, emaciated under his robes, on a sectional couch. "Human destiny," the ascetic said, "it is as a field sown with misfortune." As he spoke, the ascetic swept the air with his bony hand and smiled benignly. His words lilted with the cheerful inflections of a British Indian accent. Admittedly, the idea of Fate seems freighted for a trial such as head lice, but if God is in the details, then so, assuredly, is the devil. How else to explain the ingenious small torture of a misplaced eyelash? A paper cut? The amount of damage to the foot's naked sole wrought by a single piece of Lego?

Upstairs, my daughter dries her eyes and gets a new book while I check on my son in his room, his blond head bent over a box of football cards.

"It's not my turn," he says, not looking up.

"Not yet," I agree.

Back at the kitchen table, I find myself trying to penetrate the mysterious superiority of these two women who refuse tea, water, Christmas cookies, an invitation to use the bathroom. "Have you ever caught lice?" I ask, groping for small talk rather than the faux pas I end up making. Though I hurry to qualify the question—"From your work, I mean?"—neither woman answers. The apprentice is silent, as she has been all afternoon; the nitpicker returns to my daughter's head.

"No," she says several minutes later, and she says no more.

Although I know myself to be a person who can sit at a quiet task for long periods, by the third hour I, too, feel ready to whine and stamp my feet, and when the mail arrives I jump up to retrieve it, grateful for any diversion. After perusing the pile of catalogues and holiday cards I pass them on to my daughter, who seizes a photo greeting and Xeroxed newsletter from a family we dislike. With delighted malice she reads aloud the litany of the siblings' accomplishments. Black-belted chess champions, they study Sanskrit on Monday, harpsichord on Tuesday, underwater yoga on Wednesday. For Christmas vacation, the same that we've devoted to scratching, weeping, and surreptitiously examining our private parts, they traveled to the Third World to rebuild the governments and sewer systems of all the islands of the Malay Archipelago. My daughter and I make catty remarks about each boast, the disapproving expression of the nitpicker encouraging my guilty laughter. Still, when my daughter shreds the photograph and wishes a headful of nits on the sister she particularly dislikes, I catch an unsuppressed and quite unchristian twitch of amusement that momentarily rumples the nitpicker's purse of concentration. The fourth hour devolves into a gleeful recitation of the names of all the unlikable children we know, as we distort their juvenile failings into Roald Dahl–like extremes and punish them with amounts of nits calibrated to their crimes.

When my daughter is at last deloused and denitted, her hair is thoroughly oiled with a product that smells like citronella. I ask its ingredients, and the nitpicker sighs so gustily that I relieve her of the obligation to answer. "I know," I say. "Only the doctor knows."

Now that it's her brother's turn, my daughter sits beside me, eager to witness an equal measure of suffering. But, alas, his hair is short, his tribulations disappointingly brief. Worse, his golden hair commands grudging admiration from the two women, who smile and sigh with pleasure as it parts under the skewer.

Within an hour, he is released and it's my turn to sit in the chair under the bright bulb. The special pregnant women's solution is a sticky gel rather than a soap, and its properties do not make for smooth combing. How many years has it been since I've been handled with such rough maternal authority? I find the shampoo both extreme and humiliating in its aggression, the rinse in the kitchen sink similarly punitive, stinging suds washing into my eyes. Here is another instance that proves how routinely adults require children to soldier through discomforts they themselves rarely tolerate. One CD-ROM for each hour my daughter endured, I determine, cringing under the nitpicker's attentions—but we have to postpone our trip to J&R until tomorrow, I tell her.

"No!" she says. "Please!"

"Honey, the store closes at seven."

"Please," she begs one last time, but her tone is resigned. How can she hope to triumph over the combined authority of clock and nitpicker, both hanging over her mother's head? She sits down, allows herself to be mollified by the extravagant winces of pain I make in response to the nitpicker's attentions.

When Colin arrives home from work—punctual, as he promised in response to these blighted circumstances—he is the last of our family to submit to a head check, sitting under the light with good-humored tolerance, tilting his head agreeably and posing the kind of disarming questions I never think to ask.

"Let's see—have you ever had to delouse a man with a toupee?" he asks, and the dour woman laughs. No, but she has discovered lice on a man with a hairpiece sewn into his scalp.

"What did you do?"

"I called the office. I told the doctor I'm not—I won't handle this." And ditto for the man with recent hair implants. She laughs harder, perhaps at the idea of thousands of dollars worth of the little plugs yielding to the head-jerking comb, popping out with juicy abandon.

How sensibly my husband seems to navigate life, how naturally he puts people at their ease. Had he been home with us today, perhaps the nitpicker would have laughed all along. She pronounces Colin's enviably thick hair vermin-free and, catching my incredulous look—not that I've looked forward to his being subjected to this costly punishment, not *exactly*—she smiles. "The fathers," she says, "they never get them."

"But why?" I ask. Why should they escape? She shrugs, continuing to smile mysteriously, almost conspiratorially, as she and her apprentice pack up the bottles, the lamp, the cloth. With enchanted speed, the room is restored.

She looks up, mischievous, as she slips my check into her folder. "Ask the lice," she says. "Only he know."

LABOR

It's 3:46 when the contractions begin. Or perhaps I've been having them for a while, but the one at 3:46 is strong enough to wake me. I sit up on my elbows and watch the luminous blue face of the clock on the dresser. The six changes to a seven, the contraction ebbs, I lie back down. Beside me, Colin sleeps with a kind of heavy determination, a pillow pulled over his head, his breathing deep and measured: sandbagging in anticipation of infancy's imminent assault on our peaceful nights.

The contraction that woke me is followed by a fit of shivering. Maybe this isn't just another Braxton-Hicks. Despite the fact that we're expecting our third child, the past week has been marked by the kind of confusion that first-time mothers more usually report. Both previous labors began unambiguously, with my water breaking, followed by regular, painful contractions exactly four minutes apart—nothing to second-guess, apart from the quickest route to the hospital. But for the last few days I've had spells of regular contractions that lasted just long enough that I looked up the doctor's phone number; then they abated.

3:52, 3:58, 4:04. Six minutes apart, but are they painful, or just uncomfortable? The only thing that distinguishes them, really, is the shivering, as if my body understood what my mind confounds. I get up to pee and then, wide awake, decide to take a bath, surprised yet again at the sight of my naked self in the mirror, the unfurled navel, the expanse of taut white skin traced with blue veins. With my hands on my sides I can feel as a contraction moves through me, starting in the small of my back, sending sharp pains from my groin down the insides of my thighs, then reaching around to my front. The force of muscle flexing apart from my will, rendering my flanks as unyielding as wood, is both thrilling and a little scary. Those of us who are blessed with good health spend most of our lives assuming, mistakenly, that the mind directs the body.

A travel alarm sits on the bathroom shelf, and I watch it from the tub. 4:22, 4:28, 4:34, 4:40, 4:46. Regular, and yet no sense of real urgency. I towel off. Dressed and downstairs, I make a cup of tea and read a magazine at the dining table, filling the margins of a subscription card with notations of the time of contractions. Later we'll tear out the card and save it: a memento of our daughter's arrival.

When I return to the bedroom, up a long flight of stairs, I sit panting in the armchair by the window and watch the light as it gathers, gilding the ornate cornices of the houses to our west. Across the street, it is possible to see pigeons roosting along a ledge just under the neighbor's eaves, their heads buried in breast feathers. Across the room, Colin sits up suddenly and the blankets fall around him. He sees me in the chair, or perhaps just my ghostly silhouette, for he looks to his right and pats the bedclothes to confirm that I'm not there beside him. "Is this it?" he says, his voice thick but alert, primed for action. "This is it, isn't it?"

"I think so. I'm pretty sure."

Still, I wait until 7:00 to phone our obstetrician, the doctor who delivered both older children and who promised, whether or not on call, to deliver our third. Given the relative mildness of the contractions, we agree to meet at the hospital at 9:00, allowing us enough time for a typical school morning. Rather than distracting me, the onset of labor heightens my awareness of the familiar: the sleep-heavy limbs of our ten-year-old daughter as she submits to a hug, the wild tousled hair hanging over her younger brother's eyes while he scans the sports page, the smell of toast toasting, coffee brewing, the cat's nimble choreography around the stove burners, the dog's nose lifted in moist anticipation. On the threshold of childbirth, drawing near to that mysterious portal through which we enter life, I stand at the kitchen counter making school lunches, spreading peanut butter on slices of bread. Even sensations as small and ordinary as the sound of a new jar lid yielding—that tiny gasp of the vacuum giving way and the color of strawberry preserves beneath it—are enough to provoke tears. It's as if each contraction pushes me, as well as the baby, that much further into the world.

En route to the hospital, we drop the children off at school, answering their anxious silence with smiles and chatter, a performance that fails to reassure. They hesitate on the curb, staring at their mother, her once-familiar body gone, and the new one initiating yet another profound and disturbing change. "Go on," we tell them, "or you'll be late. Perhaps by the time you come home, you'll have a little sister."

And by now the contractions are more businesslike. When Colin takes a picture outside the entrance to the hospital I manage a smile, but a strained one. Upstairs, after signing a form and trading my clothes for a hospital gown, I try, as uselessly as I did the two previous times, to talk my way out of the enema. The labor nurse, a head higher than I, with strong arms and competent-looking hands, smiles with the kind of indulgence reserved for balky toddlers. But, secretly, I'm relieved to be bossed by this benign governess, someone who seems capable of shepherding me through whatever's to come. When she returns with the enema equipment, Colin and I exchange faces of mock terror, my husband's more genuinely mocking than mine, and agree that this might present a good interlude for him to go out for coffee.

By 11:00 an intravenous drip of the hormone Pitocin has been administered to intensify a labor that is not progressing—after seven hours I'm still at two centimeters, no more dilated than I was at my last office visit—and the doctor has broken my water with what looks like a long crochet hook, an implement he manipulates with the kind of dexterity that comes only after decades of practice. Inside me, the membrane gives way with a little snap, like that of a rubber band breaking; although I can't say if the sensation is one I hear or only feel. The gush of fluid, immediate, copious, reminds me with a visceral jolt of wetting my bed as a child, sudden heat spilling over my thighs and waking me, startled and ashamed, from the prosaic dream of going to the bathroom and pulling down underpants. Without a cushion of fluid, the baby's head grinds into my pelvis with each contraction, hard enough that I can taste the sensation; a tang of pain wells strangely from under my tongue. The nurse pulls one and then another sodden pad out from under me.

Sitting up with my knees bent, wearing an external fetal monitor secured around my middle with Velcro straps, I listen with my husband to the sound of our baby's heartbeat, quick and even, as it fills the room, speeding up at the peaking clench of each contraction. Pitocin and the breaking of the water conspire to produce contractions so intense that they no longer feel muscular but metallic. They don't ache so much as descend with a weight like that of an anvil or even an ax head, a heavy blade that drops into my pelvis and delivers me into the kind of torment that requires a considered mental stance. Why didn't I review the handouts from our old Lamaze classes instead of assuming that I'd remember the breathing tricks? Why didn't I bring a focus object? A tennis ball for backaches, a lollipop to suck? And yet, had we ever used so laughable a little arsenal? After the desultory approach of a labor that allowed for the distractions of word games and phone calls, a few entertaining bits of gossip that Colin saved for just this occasion, I've arrived at a more animal place: dark, red, claustrophobic. At the peak of a contraction I feel as if it's not just the baby who is entering the birth canal but her mother as well, labor a huge fist that tightens around me, hot and dire. The only thing that makes it bearable are the breaks between contractions, breaks that have been shortened by Pitocin.

"Talk to me. Make me laugh," I implore, and Colin says something that's funny—inside my head I recognize the humor—but distant, like a joke being told in another room. I don't smile. "What time is it?" I ask. "One o'clock," Colin says. He squeezes my foot. "You're getting there," he says, answering the real question.

The doctor puts his head in the door and, seeing the expression on my face, offers a guess as to how many centimeters: eight. He confirms his suspicion with an exam and then exchanges the external fetal monitor, which keeps slipping off the steep slope of my belly, for an internal one, its eavesdropping electrode applied directly to the baby's scalp. Now our daughter's heartbeat has a crisper, clearer cadence; she seems that much closer to arriving. Colin and I hold hands, and I look at his face, trying to measure my pain in his eyes.

My reasons for rejecting anesthesia are complex. It's not only that I'm an experience junkie, someone who regards labor as a kind of domestic Everest to scale and who doesn't want any separation from the adventure that painkillers would grant. Raised as a Christian Scientist, I'm a past master at denying all forms of discomfort, and the idea of enduring childbirth without drugs offers both the temptation of a spiritual test as well as a correction to the cerebral double-talk of a faith I ultimately rejected as magical thinking. All this notwithstanding, as I enter transition—those last two centimeters of cervical dilation just before the head moves into the birth canal—I'm panicking at the idea of pain this bad getting worse.

Transition is, demonstrably, a local process and affects a limited part of my body. Still, it's so intense that it seems bigger than the whole of me—bigger than the bed, the doctor, the equipment. Instead of it being in me, I am in it, a seascape I traverse: all of me struggling to swim through rogue waves, to keep my head above violent black water. I stop being aware of the room as a cohesive whole, experiencing only flashes of my environment: light gleaming on the chrome bed rail, the bottom slat of the window blind grazing the sill, the latch on a cabinet, the clear visor attached to the doctor's surgical mask. The contents of the room are fractured and refracted, like the subject of a Cubist painting, breaking up under the pressure. As each contraction begins I try to find one detail and hold it before me, prevent myself from closing my eyes because when I do, when it's black, pain closes over my head.

And there's not enough time to rest, to breathe, to gather myself; contractions are coming too fast, one on top of another, tidal, my body breaking up along with the room, flotsam. And I remember, yes, this is what I was frightened of. In those few seconds that I allowed myself to acknowledge fear, the moments when the veil of Christian Science and all other apparatuses of denial slipped, this is what I saw approaching—black, and so much bigger than I.

One centimeter to go and the baby is slightly transverse. The labor nurse directs me to lie on my left side, to turn my body and thereby bring our child's into place for delivery. I nod up at her face, impossibly calm, smiling, but don't move, so she hauls me over by my right arm and I stay there by holding on to the bed rail. The next contraction is so crushing that I wrench my shoulder pulling at the chrome rail. A week later the pulled muscles will be so sore that I can't pick up a hairbrush, but in the moment I feel nothing in my shoulder; I'm wholly occupied by the impossible rending of my pelvis, silently repeating and repeating what has become my stunned mantra: It can't last forever, it can't last forever, it feels like it will, but it can't last much longer.

The fetal monitor is removed for delivery and the cessation of the broadcast of that fast little heartbeat is startling: how used we'd grown to what we'd taken as her voice, and how silent it seems without her clapping us on. I'm caught between a desire to push, to have it over with, and an equal desire to stay very still, to keep holding tight to the bed rail, the fingers, the frayed plaid cuff of Colin's shirt, whatever little handhold might offer another second's purchase before I drop back into agony. At the onset of each contraction three people—husband, doctor, and nurse—tell me to push, all three cheer me on, flog me on, and I do push, obedient because I know it's the only way toward release, the only means of escape. In between pushes, the baby's head emerging slowly—how can it be so slow?—I feel no relief, just bewil-

derment that so impossible a posture is sustainable for minutes on end.

The polite woman I used to be has departed, frightened
off by my wild, animal howls—embarrassing, if I weren't so
far from embarrassment. How is it that this morning I was
dressed, upright, articulate, and now I'm half naked, one
foot planted in the nurse's open palm, the other on the doctor's chest, and screaming loud enough to frighten women in
adjacent rooms? Everything is pulsing black and red, and
the only thing I want is to be rescued, the only words I say
are *help me*. More usually possessed of the kind of morbid cu-
riosity that peers into dark places, now I'm glad I can't see
what feels like the rupture of every organ. Eyes screwed
shut, ears popping and squeaking, stomach acid forced into
my throat, it takes eight pushing contractions to deliver the
baby, the last, at 2:20, accompanied by an awful burning as
one little shoulder tears its way into the world, followed by
the blessedly swift, wet, and slithering arrival of the rest of
her—fast, so fast, after the slow agonies of the last hours.
The placenta, too, almost seems to fall out of me, with a
speed that is unnerving, as if, having opened this rent between my legs, everything else will drop out: heart and lungs
and soul.

But the baby is in my hands, and my husband takes a picture as I start to weep. How beautiful she is in her cloak of
red and white, a royal robe of blood and vernix, her eyes
shocked squinting slits, her lashes matted, skin a mauve so
perfect, so fantastic—a color I have never seen before. Like a
paper flower dropped into a bowl of water, she has unfolded,
but not completely; we see the posture she held for so many
months. Seven pounds and four ounces, a whole pound
smaller than her brother, how is it that she seemed so large,
undeliverable? Next to the bed the placenta lies in a blue
plastic dish, gleaming and fat with secret knowledge, mar-

velous in its symmetry. I'm overwhelmed by a paradox of pride and humility: what a gorgeous thing I've accomplished, and how little credit I can take for it.

Three times now it's been true what they say: yes, it hurt more than can be imagined, and already, examining the minute perfection of each nail and cuticle, I've forgotten.

MOTHER'S DAY
CARD

I still dream of you, Mother, and how beautiful you look. Thick dark hair that catches the sunlight, cheeks as pale and smooth as a funerary angel's, eyes that smolder with misery, lips painted with promises: cosmetics can't achieve the kind of glamour you command. It's you in your twenty-fifth year, seen through my starstruck seven-year-old eyes, and even in sleep, I'm paralyzed by desire. How can I hold you? How can I keep you? I wake exhausted from the excitement of your presence.

Long ago, love made me a beggar, grateful for a glimpse, a touch, the hem of your dress brushing past. Because I've missed you all my life, your death feels, perhaps, less awful than another mother's might to another daughter. I tell myself it does. After all, I'm used to my longing.

When he was small, our son—your grandson—used to confuse the word *love* with *miss*. At bedtime, he would take my face in his hands. "I miss you!" he'd say, his voice ragged with passion.

"I'm right here," I'd answer. "I'm right here with you." I couldn't correct him. Hadn't he, after all, gotten it right?

When you died, this is what I said to myself: It's over. At twenty-four, I was young enough to imagine that death would mark the end of our relationship. I'd looked forward to your dying; it seemed the one thing that might release us both—you from cancer, me from a vigil that began with my birth.

"*Hostage,*" you called me. The word you wanted was *surrogate,* but you were in a hurry. We were driving through Coldwater Canyon, about to arrive at the end of the conversation. I was twelve and you were trying once again to explain how things were the way they were. What had happened was this: You'd given me to your mother. I was the price of your freedom, I was all you'd had to offer. But at eighteen you didn't know what a baby was worth, didn't know that you'd just rearranged the terms of your own captivity. *Hostage.* I said the word silently to myself until the syllables collapsed into nonsense.

After your death, when I didn't know what a mother was worth, I determined that you would remain the only one to have brought me to my knees, to have made me beg. Not in front of you, never in front of you—I had my pride—but you knew that every star wished on, every prayer whispered, every candle lit, was yours. A ransom's worth.

After your death, I tried to imagine what the circumstances might be that could tempt me back into a posture of supplication. As it's turned out, I bow my head eagerly. Each night, by their beds, knees mortified by Lego, elbows planted among stuffed animals, I'm being rehabilitated.

Your grandson no longer mistakes *miss* for *love.* And, as for your daughter, she's making progress, too.

ACKNOWLEDGMENTS

The author wishes to thank Amy Benfer, Bill Buford, Charis Conn, Sharon and Steve Fiffer, Courtney Hodell, Barbara Jones, David Kuhn, Josh Lerman, Dan Max, Kate Medina, Cathleen Medwick, Ben Metcalf, Lorie Parch, Mickey Pearlman, Ph.D., Christopher Potter, Elissa Schappell, Ilena Silverman, Robert Spillman, Mary Turner, and Amanda Urban.

And, last but never least, thanks to Colin: husband-editor-best friend, collaborator on everything I hold dear.

ABOUT THE TYPE

This book was set in Granjon, a modern recutting of a typeface produced under the direction of George W. Jones, who based Granjon's design upon the letter forms of Claude Garamond (1480–1561). The name was given to the typeface as a tribute to the typographic designer Robert Granjon.

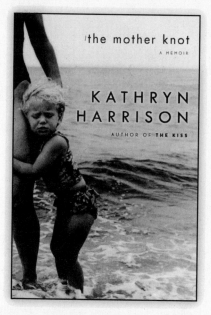